W9-AWC-095

Bicycling Fuel

Bicycling Fuel

Nutrition for Bicycle Riders

Richard Rafoth, MD

Bicycle Books – San Francisco

Copyright © Richard Rafoth, 1988, 1989, 1993
Third, revised and expanded edition, 1993

Printed in the United States of America

Cover photograph by Stief
Diagrams by Rob van der Plas

Published by:
Bicycle Books, Inc.
PO Box 2038
Mill Valley CA 94942

Distributed to the book trade by:
USA   National Book Network, Lanham, MD
UK: Chris Lloyd Sales and Marketing, Poole, Dorset
Canada: Raincoast Book Distribution, Vancouver, BC

Cataloging in Publication Data:
Rafoth, Richard, 1945 –
Bicycling Fuel, Nutrition for bicycle riders
Third, revised and expanded edition
Bibliography: p. Includes index
1. Nutrition, handbooks, manuals, etc.
2. Bicycles and bicycling, handbooks, manuals, etc.
Authorship—handbooks, manuals, etc.
I. Title

Library of Congress Catalog Card Number 92-83824

ISBN 0-933201-54-0 Paperback original

Acknowledgements

Many thanks to Ms. Cathy Markham, RD, for her constructive comments and suggestions.

The original idea for this book was born and nurtured on the long training rides for a double century (a 200-mile ride). Those of us with a scientific bent were convinced that there must be solid research detailing the optimal diet for training and racing. Although my original literature search identified a number of papers on basic physiology, there were few of practical value. On the other hand, there were numerous anecdotes, personal opinions, and unsupported recommendations ranging from the need to carbo-load for a one-hour recreational ride to the advantages of fats and alcohol in training diets. The first edition attempted to bridge this gap with recommendations based on the few scientific studies available.

When I returned to the literature this year, I was pleased to find a number of papers addressing our original questions. In addition, there were several in-depth studies on triathletes and Tour de France participants. I was happy to find that the majority of the original assumptions and recommendations had been validated, although there was a need for some fine tuning here and there. The most exciting discovery, however, was that this edition could now address in full the concerns of both the ultra-endurance athlete and the recreational rider.

Table of Contents

Richard Rafoth, MD, is a specialist in diseases of the digestive tract (gastroenterology) and practices in Everett, Washington. Among his hobbies are outdoor physical activities, including cross-country skiing, long-distance running, and cycling.

While preparing with a group of cyclists for the Seattle to Portland Bicycle Classic, a two-hundred-mile ride held each June, the issue of nutrition was a frequent topic of discussion during group training rides. Noting the variety of approaches to nutritional conditioning and the many misconceptions, Dr. Rafoth began to search for a book containing the appropriate facts to set the group straight.

The idea for the present book was born when he failed to find an existing text that was both medically correct and practically oriented. Dr. Rafoth hopes this book will strike the balance between basic physiologic principles and practical application of sound nutritional principles when preparing for, and participating in, cycling events.

CHAPTER 1

Basic Physiology

Aside from being a pleasant diversion for the cyclist, food is a necessity that provides the energy required to move man and machine. In this opening section we will discuss the principles of digestion, absorption, and metabolism to convert food energy into a form that can be used by the muscle cells. When appropriate, the physiology of exercise will be discussed, emphasizing important points for the cyclist.

The Raw Materials

All foods are composed of carbohydrates, fats, and protein. Carbohydrates are the primary energy source for the average recreational cyclist and all athletes involved in short, maximum-performance events. Fats, which can also serve as an energy source, assume more importance in endurance events. Proteins are used to maintain and repair cells throughout the body.

Food energy is released through a chemical reaction with oxygen in a process called oxidation. When this occurs outside the body—for example, the burning of oil (a fat) in a lamp or the use of a flaming sugar cube (a carbohydrate) as a decoration on a dessert—this energy is released as heat and light. In the body, however, food energy needs to be released more slowly and in a form that can be harnessed for basic cell functions and transformed into mechanical movement by the muscle cells.

This is accomplished by "refining" the three basic food materials into a single common chemical compound, adenosine triphosphate or ATP. It is ATP, produced through the metabolism of the fats, carbohydrates, and proteins in our diet, that transfers food energy to the muscles.

The energy contained in equal weights of carbohydrate, fat, and protein varies. It is measured in Calories, or Cal, (in the American system of units) or kilojoules, or kJ, (in the international, or scientific, system of units—see Appendix B for an explanation and the relevant conversion factors). The energy in one nutritional

Calorie (note the uppercase C) is the equivalent of a kilocalorie, i.e., 1,000 calories (lower case c), or 4.18 kilojoules. Carbohydrates and protein both contain 4.1 Calories per gram (120 Calories per ounce), while fat contains about twice as many for an equivalent weight. The customary abbreviations for the various units discussed here are listed below:

Calorie:	Cal	=	4.18 kJ
kilocalorie:	kcal	=	4.18 kJ
calorie:	cal	=	4.18 J
joule:	J	=	0.24 cal
kilojoule:	kJ	=	1000 J

Digestion

Digestion is the physical and chemical alteration of food to allow absorption by the cells of the intestinal tract. These mechanical and chemical changes occur equally in the stomach and the small intestine, but all absorption takes place in the small intestine.

Let's take a look at the digestive process with particular attention to those aspects that are important to the cyclist. Figure 1.1, which schematically represents the digestive tract, will be helpful as a reference.

The first step in digestion is mechanical disruption, which allows digestive enzymes to reach the individual food molecules to begin the chemical changes required for absorption by the cells of the small intestine. This begins with chewing and continues with the muscular churning of the stomach, where most of the mechanical modification takes place. The mechanical phase of digestion is completed as this semiliquid material, called chyme, proceeds through the small intestine (comprising the duodenum, jejunum, and ileum as shown in the illustration).

The next step is the chemical processing of the larger food molecules by digestive enzymes secreted into the chyme by stomach, pancreas, and small intestinal cells. Only then can absorption by small intestinal lining cells take place.

The time needed for the stomach to complete its work and empty its contents into the small intestine is modified by several factors. Because absorption takes place only in the small intestine, these factors directly affect how quickly the food eaten will be

made available to the muscle as ATP. The cyclist can control four
of these factors:

1. the form of food (solid or liquid);

2. the fat content of food;

3. the concentration of sugar in food;

4. the physical activity level of the cyclist.

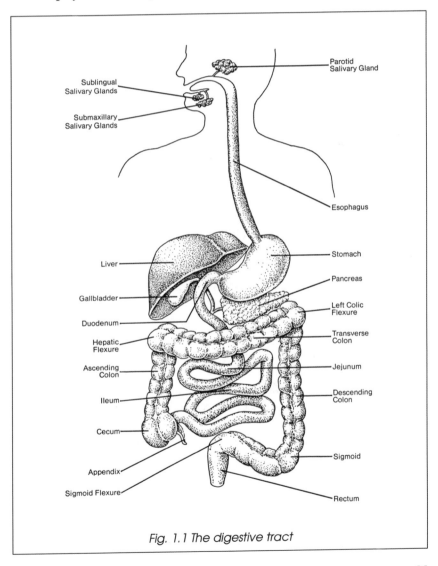

Fig. 1.1 The digestive tract

The more liquid a food, the faster it is emptied from the stomach. Although chewing can be of some help, it is the initial form of the food—liquid or solid—that is most important. Physiologic studies have shown that it takes up to 4 hours for a solid meal to be mechanically altered and emptied from the stomach, while 75% of a meal that is already in liquid form when it is consumed will be completely emptied into the small intestine within an hour.[31]

Fat in food slows down the emptying of the stomach. As a result, a solid food with a moderate fat content empties more slowly than a lean or non-fatty one. Likewise, fatty liquids empty more slowly than those that are fat-free. However, a liquid with some fat will empty more quickly than a low-fat, solid food, which must first be mechanically altered by the stomach.

A high sugar content also slows stomach emptying. The same characteristics of the small intestine that allow food molecules to pass into the body also allow water from the body to be drawn into the intestinal tract when a concentrated solution is present. To protect the body from rapid fluid shifts and dehydration, the stomach slows the emptying rate of very concentrated sugar solutions into the small intestine. The concentration of sugar molecules in solution is referred to as its osmotic activity. The more molecules present in a given volume, the more osmotically active the solution, and the greater its effect to slow gastric emptying.

This is a problem for the competitive athlete who wants to maximize his or her energy intake but doesn't need the associated volume of fluid necessary to maintain the sugar concentration at the optimum for the most rapid emptying of the stomach. The answer to this dilemma is the fact that the stomach interprets concentration as the *number of molecules*—regardless of their size—that are present in a specific volume of liquid. If several molecules of sugar (glucose) are linked together, a single complex carbohydrate molecule results, which contains the energy equivalent of the several original glucose molecules but affects osmotic activity as a single molecule. Thus, by using complex carbohydrates, more molecules of glucose can be delivered to the small intestine with a given volume of fluid than is possible with a simple glucose solution.

Finally, the mechanical activity throughout the entire digestive tract is slowed by vigorous physical work or exercise. A fast walk resulting in a heart rate of 108 bpm (beats/min) was shown to decrease stomach emptying and intestinal absorption by almost 40% in one study.[16] In another, it was demonstrated that above 70% of a person's physical functional capacity (V_{O2max}), there is a progressive slowing of stomach activity until muscular activity stops and no emptying occurs.[6] Fortunately, except for competitive events, cycling does not require the level of exertion that results in this more dramatic effect on the intestinal tract.

Once you understand these factors that affect stomach emptying, decisions on snacks can be made based on the type of ride planned and the anticipated urgency of the caloric replacement. When a quick energy boost is needed during the ride, a semiliquid to liquid simple carbohydrate with minimal fat content is ideal. However, steady intake is necessary as the stomach rapidly empties and the body is once again dependent on its own internal energy reserves. The endurance rider, on the other hand, might prefer a complex carbohydrate in a more solid form that will empty from the stomach and be absorbed over a longer period of time. A small amount of fat will also help to prolong the digestive and absorptive process, providing extra Calories (fats contain twice as many Calories per gram as carbohydrates) and improving the taste.

Carbohydrates

Carbohydrates are the major dietary energy source for most adults, providing from 40% to 60% of the daily energy requirements. During exercise the metabolism of the muscle cells shifts; carbohydrates become even more important as a fuel source. An understanding of their absorption and metabolism is essential in developing a program to maximize performance.

The basic building blocks of all carbohydrates are single sugar molecules, or monosaccharides. Glucose and fructose are the two most common monosaccharides in our diet. The linking of two monosaccharides results in a disaccharide, while long chains of sugar molecules are referred to as complex carbohydrates, or polysaccharides.

Most dietary carbohydrate comes from the disaccharides sucrose (or cane sugar), and lactose (or milk sugar), and from complex carbohydrates, called starches, primarily supplied by grains. Before they can be absorbed from the intestinal tract, all disaccharides and complex carbohydrates must first be converted back to the monosaccharide, or single molecule, form.

Digestion of complex carbohydrates begins in the stomach, where salivary enzymes, mixed with food during chewing, convert up to 40% of dietary starch into disaccharide form. The remainder is broken down in the upper small intestine by pancreatic enzymes. The final step in this process, the reduction to monosaccharides, is the result of enzymes secreted by the lining cells of the small intestine.

After monosaccharides are absorbed by the small intestine, they are transported throughout the body via the circulatory system. After absorption into a cell, they can be metabolized immediately to release energy, or they can be stored in the form of glycogen, a complex carbohydrate polymer of numerous glucose molecules. Liver and muscle cells are the major storage sites for glycogen. The average 160-pound person has approximately 365 grams of carbohydrate, stored as:

liver glycogen:	110 grams
muscle glycogen:	245 grams
extracellular blood sugar:	10 grams

These 365 grams contain almost 1,500 Calories of energy, which equals several hours of cycling at a brisk pace or one hour of out-and-out racing.

Almost all movement of glucose from the bloodstream, through the cell wall membrane and into the cell, is controlled by the hormone insulin, produced by specialized cells in the pancreas. Although some glucose can enter the cell without insulin, the rate of transfer increases 25 times when insulin is present. In fact, without insulin the rate of movement into the cell is so slow that there would not be enough energy available to meet the minimal energy requirements to sustain life.

Vigorous physical exercise promotes the movement of glucose into muscle cells by increasing the permeability of the cell membrane to glucose and by increasing the sensitivity to insulin. During exercise, blood insulin levels have been shown to drop to 50% of their resting level. Although this is not a factor in normal daily activities, it is important for the athlete.

Insulin is released by the pancreatic cells when there is a rise in the blood sugar (glucose) level from intestinal absorption. This in turn leads to an increased movement of glucose from the blood-stream into the body cells, preventing an excessive rise in the blood sugar level. Any excess glucose not needed for immediate cell energy requirements is stored as glycogen.

An understanding of the relationship between food absorption, insulin release, and glucose uptake by the cells is important in planning pre-event nutrition for athletes. If a small amount of glucose in an easily absorbed form, such as a sugar drink, is ingested, it will be emptied quickly from the stomach and absorbed. This leads to a rise in blood sugar and release of insulin by the pancreatic cells. However, with a pure sugar solution—containing only sucrose and water—the duration of the insulin effect persists beyond the availability of further glucose from intestinal absorption. This results in a drop in the blood sugar level, which will be accentuated by exercise.

When the blood sugar drops below a critical level, it is referred to as hypoglycemia and is accompanied by weakness and poor athletic performance. To prevent hypoglycemia, the cyclist should avoid high-sugar foods or liquids for at least one hour prior to exercising. Another alternative is to eat complex carbohydrates, which will be emptied from the stomach and absorbed more slowly, moderating swings in blood sugar levels.

During exercise, on the other hand, sugar solutions have a positive effect on performance. Exercise increases the movement of blood sugar into the cell, blunting the rise in the blood sugar level from intestinal absorption; insulin release is prevented or minimized; and an overcorrection of the blood sugar level with a drop to hypoglycemic levels does not occur.

Most glucose is metabolized through oxygen-dependent, or aerobic, biochemical processes. These are very efficient, with 39% of the energy contained in the glucose molecule being available to the cell via ATP for specific cell functions (the remainder is lost as heat). If the circulatory system is unable to meet the oxygen demands of the muscles during strenuous exercise, oxygen-independent, or anaerobic, metabolism takes over. Anaerobic metabolism is not only less efficient, with only 2% of the food energy being available to the cells, but also leads to the formation of lactic acid, which has a negative effect on muscle performance.

Fats

Fats provide 20%–40% of the Calories in the average American diet. About 95% of dietary fat is in the form of triglycerides, which are composed of a glycerol molecule and three fatty acid (FA) molecules. The other 5% is cholesterol and phospholipids. Whereas cholesterol and phospholipids are essential building blocks for cell growth, triglycerides are used primarily as an energy source. They are very important to the endurance cyclist, but play only a minor role in short distance, maximum performance events.

Essentially all fat digestion occurs in the small intestine, with bile from the liver aiding enzymes from the pancreas. The individual fatty acid molecules are cleaved from the glycerol backbone to become free fatty acids, or FFA. The FFA are then absorbed by the cells lining the small intestine, moved into the lymph system, and are ultimately emptied into the circulatory system. They are then distributed throughout the body and diffused through cell membranes, where they are metabolized as an immediate energy source or stored after reconstitution to the triglyceride form. Any excess dietary carbohydrate is also converted into triglycerides for storage after the body's glycogen stores have been completely filled.

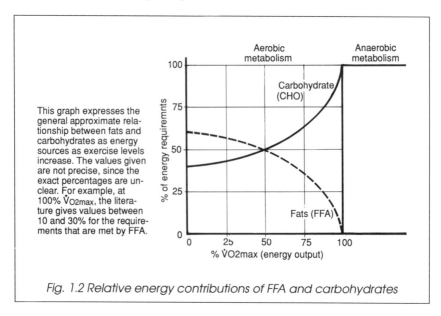

This graph expresses the general approximate relationship between fats and carbohydrates as energy sources as exercise levels increase. The values given are not precise, since the exact percentages are unclear. For example, at 100% $\dot{V}O_{2}max$, the literature gives values between 10 and 30% for the requirements that are met by FFA.

Fig. 1.2 Relative energy contributions of FFA and carbohydrates

As energy demands increase, the reverse process occurs: triglycerides are broken down into individual fatty acids (FFA), transported to the cells where they are needed, and used as an energy source. As this takes place after glycogen stores have been depleted, it is especially important in endurance athletic events.

Protein

Protein is the third major food component and provides approximately 20% of our daily caloric intake. Its role is to provide the building blocks for cell formation and repair. Detailed studies have shown that the oxidation of protein provides less than 5% of the energy expended during exercise, and it appears that only during starvation or extreme malnutrition is it used as a source of energy for normal cell functions.[50, 52]

The building blocks of proteins are single-molecule components called amino acids. Protein digestion begins in the stomach with enzymes secreted by the stomach lining cells and is completed in the small intestine by enzymes from the pancreas and small intestinal cells. Once digestion has produced free amino acids, they are absorbed by the small intestinal lining cells, transported by the blood, and are removed by individual body cells.

Of the 20 amino acids needed for cell growth and survival, 11 can be synthesized within the cells of the human body and are referred to as nonessential amino acids. The other 9, which are essential to cell survival, must be provided by the diet. Both meat and vegetables are good sources of protein; however, animal proteins contain a better balance of essential and nonessential amino acids. Vegetarians must eat a larger variety of foods to assure that their amino acid requirements are met, being careful that these proteins "complement" each other to supply all the essential amino acids.

Each individual cell has an upper limit for protein storage. When this limit is reached, excess amino acids are transformed into triglycerides or glycogen. In other words, high protein intake does not automatically result in additional muscle (cell) formation but instead is converted to fat. Studies with athletes have indicated that 1.2 grams of protein per kg of body weight per day are adequate for muscle development in most sports, and even in strength training, protein in excess of 2 g/kg/day will be turned into fat.

The Muscle

Initial sections of this chapter have focused on the three food types available to the cyclist as energy sources, and have emphasized the unique metabolic characteristics that affect their use in a high-performance dietary program. Now it is time to look at the "engine" that converts this energy to mechanical performance: the cyclist's muscles.

As with any other engine, the efficiency of the human muscle is measured as the percentage of energy input that is converted to actual mechanical work. Under optimal conditions, the muscle converts 20%–25% of the chemical energy available in the foods we eat into physical performance. The rest is released as heat.

Skeletal muscle makes up over half of the body weight in a lean individual. These muscle cells contain two proteins—actin and myosin—which chemically interact to shorten the muscle fiber when stimulated by nerve impulses. This process requires energy provided by ATP.

There are two types of muscle fibers: Type I, or slow twitch; and Type II, or fast twitch. The slow twitch muscle fibers are more efficient, using both fats and carbohydrate for energy. They are the major muscle fiber in use at 70%–80% of V_{O2max}.[42] Fast twitch fibers, on the other hand, are less efficient, using mainly glycogen as fuel. They are called into action for sprints as the athlete approaches 100% of maximum performance.[23]

The carbohydrates and fats used as fuel by the muscle cells are available from reserves within the cell itself (as glycogen and triglycerides). They can also be transported to the cell via the bloodstream, either from intestinal absorption (as glucose and free fatty acids) or after mobilization from storage elsewhere in the body (liver cells and fatty or adipose tissue). Inside the muscle cell, these basic food components are metabolized to form ATP, which then powers the cellular machinery. Muscle cells contain a significant proportion of the body's glycogen stores and a small amount of triglycerides. This muscle glycogen and triglyceride offer the advantage of being immediately accessible as an energy source without the intermediate step of transportation by the circulatory system.

Oxygen Consumption

Production of ATP is most efficient when adequate oxygen is available for aerobic metabolism. Oxygen consumption, expressed as V_{O2}, reflects the amount of oxygen utilized for oxidation and energy production during a specified period of time. Maximum oxygen consumption, referred to as V_{O2max}, is an individual's upper limit of aerobic metabolism. At greater levels of exertion, the energy requirements of the cells outstrip the ability of the cardiovascular system to deliver the required oxygen, and oxygen-independent, or anaerobic, energy production begins.

V_{O2max} depends on several factors, including lung capacity, heart rate, and the ability of the muscle to extract oxygen from the blood. A rough correlation of the level of activity and percentage of V_{O2max} can be made from the heart rate alone. If the maximum heart rate (MHR) is considered as 220 minus age in years, then 60%–70% MHR = 50%–85% V_{O2max}.[42]

Training increases an individual's V_{O2max}. This is a result of an increase in the size and the number of muscle cell mitochondria, an increase in the activity of metabolic enzymes in the muscle cell, an increase in the number of capillaries that supply blood to the muscle, and an increase in the amount of blood the heart can pump (cardiac output).

Anaerobic metabolism occurs during particularly strenuous periods of activity when the cell's oxygen demands cannot be met. It is not only less efficient, with a more rapid depletion of the muscle glycogen stores, but also results in the production of lactic acid as a by-product. It is the build-up of lactic acid and other acid metabolites that ultimately limits performance, even though adequate glycogen stores may remain. The degradation of lactic acid after oxygen again becomes available is responsible for the oxygen debt or recovery phase that follows anaerobic exercise.

Recent work with endurance cyclists has focused on the blood lactate threshold (LT) as a reflection of potential performance. The lactate threshold is the percentage of V_{O2max} at which lactate begins to accumulate in the blood. It improves with training, but varies even among highly trained cyclists. It reflects exercise efficiency in that those with a higher LT use less glycogen for any level of performance and thus can exercise longer before their muscle stores are depleted.

Muscle Energy Supply and Fatigue

Although carbohydrates are the major energy source for the muscles during vigorous activity, fats (via FFA metabolism) can also be an important energy source for the working muscle under aerobic conditions. In fact, it is thought that a shift toward fat metabolism may be the physiologic explanation for the "second wind" that can occur with exercise.

Fats can provide over 50% of the Calories expended during moderate exercise, even when adequate glycogen stores are available. As V_{O2max} is approached, and anaerobic metabolism increases, the energy provided by fats diminishes to between 10% and 30% of total Calories expended. In maximum-performance events, where metabolism is entirely anaerobic, fat metabolism ceases and carbohydrates are the only energy source.[2]

When muscle glycogen has been depleted and no additional blood sugar is available, the muscle is dependent entirely on FFA for its energy supply. However, as fat is a less efficient energy

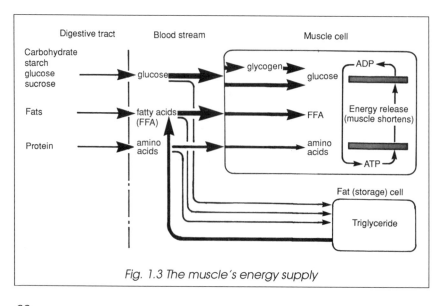

Fig. 1.3 The muscle's energy supply

source than carbohydrate, energy output can not be maintained above 60%–70% V_{O2max}.[30, 35]

Initially, the liver supplements muscle glycogen during sustained exercise by releasing glucose and maintaining a stable blood sugar level. The "bonk" occurs when liver glycogen levels are depleted. It can be avoided or cured by eating carbohydrates to maintain the blood sugar level. "Hitting the wall" is a result of depletion of both liver and muscle glycogen. Although it is avoidable, once it occurs it is impossible to reverse, and muscle energy supplies are then limited to FFA metabolism. At exhaustion, irreversible changes occur in the muscle cell itself and further competitive activity is impossible, no matter what the blood sugar level.

Next, let's look at the relative contribution of glucose and FFA to muscle energy needs relative to the phase of exercise. During prolonged aerobic performance at greater than 50% maximum oxygen uptake (but less than the 100% of maximum performance where anaerobic metabolism comes into play), three distinct phases can be identified.

During the first few minutes, before increased muscle blood flow and hormonal adaptations to exercise have occurred, glycogen is the primary fuel. As much as 20% of the total muscle glycogen stores may be consumed during this phase.

During the second phase, there is a shift in metabolism to a mixture of carbohydrate and FFA. Muscle glycogen stores continue to decrease, reflecting their ongoing utilization, but now the muscles also extract and metabolize FFA and glucose from the arterial blood supply. During moderate exercise, FFA and carbohydrates contribute equally as an energy source; at lesser intensities the ratio changes, with FFA taking on increasing importance. And, as noted above, as the anaerobic threshold is approached, the opposite shift occurs with almost all energy supplied by carbohydrate alone.

The third phase begins when muscle glycogen is completely depleted. It is at this point that a sense of fatigue occurs, exercise intensity can not be maintained, and muscle metabolism shifts almost entirely to FFA.

There are four practical points here for the cyclist. The first is that both liver and muscle glycogen support the initial phase of exercise (3–4 hours at 70% V_{O2max}), and good training as well as riding at a reasonable pace postpone the time at which glycogen is depleted and fatigue occurs. The second point is that a good oral intake of carbohydrates helps to maintain an adequate blood sugar level and provides a second source of glucose fuel. The third is the fact that even with optimal nutrition, a point is reached where exhaustion occurs and the rider has to slow down or stop.[6, 35] Finally, even though greater amounts of glycogen in the cell prior to activity can prolong the duration of that activity, it cannot increase the muscle's maximum energy output.

Muscle glycogen stores are affected by diet. On a high-carbohydrate diet the muscle glycogen content is higher than on a low- carbohydrate diet of equal caloric value. It has also been demonstrated that when muscle glycogen stores are completely depleted by exercise, there is an overcompensation when they are replaced—a rebound phenomenon. These two observations support the concept of carbohydrate loading. At its simplest, this refers to a high-carbohydrate diet for 2 or 3 days immediately prior to an event.

A more extensive carbohydrate loading program adds a preliminary depletion phase, consisting of intensive exercise and 2 or 3 days of a low-carbohydrate diet followed by 2 or 3 days of high carbohydrate intake with minimal athletic activity. This results in the maximum depletion of muscle glycogen stores and takes advantage of the rebound effect during the period of high carbohydrate consumption, leading to a muscle glycogen level 50% higher than that on a standard diet. Carbohydrate loading is discussed in more detail in Chapters 3, 4 and 5.

CHAPTER 2

Energy Requirements

The mechanical energy needed to move a cyclist a given distance is a product of the distance ridden and the energy expended per mile. Since the human "machine" is less than 100% efficient in converting food energy into mechanical energy, replacement energy requirements, in Calories, are equivalent to the mechanical energy expended divided by efficiency. This energy is supplied by the food we eat.

Energy Requirements of Cycling

Now that we've reviewed the physiology of converting food energy into muscle mechanical activity, let's review the energy requirements of cycling. This will help in planning an appropriate nutrition program.

As we discuss the energy requirements of cycling, reference will again be made to the terms Calorie and calorie. These terms not only express the energy content of different foods, but also the

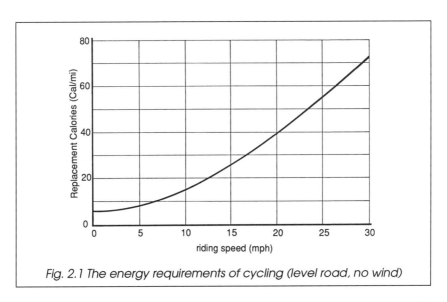

Fig. 2.1 The energy requirements of cycling (level road, no wind)

energy released by cellular metabolism and the mechanical or other physical work performed.

In physical science, a calorie is the quantity of heat required to raise the temperature of 1 gram of water 1 degree centigrade. As this unit is too small to easily express the energy utilized and expended in biologic systems, the Calorie, which is equal to 1,000 calories (or 1 kcal), is used in discussions of human energy metabolism.

In the previous chapter we learned that ATP, or adenosine triphosphate, is the common energy carrier to transfer the energy in foodstuffs to the cells. As this energy transfer takes place, large portions are lost as heat. On the average, about 60% of all the energy in the food we eat becomes heat during the process of ATP formation. Additional energy is lost, again as heat, when energy transfer takes place from ATP to muscle contraction. The result is that only 25% of the energy in food is actually available for mechanical work by the muscles.

The bicycle itself is a very efficient machine. Over 95% of the cyclist's energy is translated into forward motion and less than 5% is lost as heat due to the resistance of the bearings, rolling resistance of the tires, etc.[47]

On a level surface, aerodynamic drag, or wind resistance, consumes most of the cyclist's energy output. This aerodynamic resistance increases with the cyclist's speed relative to the mass of air through which the bicycle is moving—not relative to the ground. That is why a headwind will increase energy needs for a given ground speed, and a tailwind will decrease them.

The relationship between energy requirements and air speed is an exponential one. This means that doubling the forward speed more than doubles energy requirements. The actual relationship is illustrated in Fig. 2.1 and Table 2.3. If the terrain is not level, additional energy is required to raise bike and rider against gravity. The exact calculations are covered in Appendix A. To put it in perspective, the energy expended per mile of cycling is about one fifth that of running.

Friction

Although friction, or resistance, may be unavoidable in cycling, it can be minimized. Any improvements provide a performance edge in short, competitive events and decrease the energy needs on longer rides.

If bearings and chain are well lubricated and adjusted, they will absorb only 3%–5% of the energy output of a rider. The resistance of wheel and bottom bracket bearings can be further reduced for special events such as time trials and pursuits if the grease is removed and replaced with a light oil. However, they must be oiled frequently and oil does not give the protection from moisture and dirt provided by a coating of grease. The bicycle chain should be well worn and lubricated with a light oil. Heavier lubricants such as paraffin will last longer but cause more friction.

Rolling resistance of tires is related to the compression and expansion of the tread, casing, and sidewall as the tire rolls. It is also directly related to the size of the footprint or contact patch where the tire physically meets the road. The rolling resistance can be decreased by using a higher inflation pressure and using thinner, more flexible tires. You can usually judge the quality of a tire by pinching the casing to test its pliability. Light, thinner-walled tires and tubes are almost always better. Natural latex is more elastic than synthetic butyl rubber. Extra layers of material, belts, and liners cause more friction.

Weight

Unnecessary weight in any form is detrimental to performance and is really just a different form of resistance. The effect of weight increases dramatically with steeper slopes. Although a heavier rider can descend faster than a lighter one, this fails to make up for the time lost while climbing. This explains why lighter riders have a natural advantage on hilly stages. However, big riders should not despair, as conditioning and riding technique can offset this climbing advantage.

Rotating parts require more energy to accelerate than fixed parts. For example, it takes twice as much energy to accelerate the additional weight in a wheel rim as it does to accelerate an equal weight added to the frame. Therefore, you should upgrade to lighter tires, rims, cranksets, and shoes first.

Air Resistance and Drafting

At cycling speeds greater than 15 mph, the energy expended to overcome air resistance exceeds that required to overcome the sum of rolling and mechanical resistances. For example, when speed is increased from 7.5 mph to 20 mph, mechanical resistance increases by 225%, rolling resistance by 363%, and air resistance by 1,800%. Thus at 20 mph, two-thirds of the total energy output is necessary to overcome air resistance. This is the explanation for the energy-saving or performance advantage of drafting or using aerodynamic equipment.

A recent study nicely demonstrated that at 20 mph, drafting a single rider reduced energy requirements (measured as V_{O2}) by 18% and at 25 mph by 27%. Using aerodynamic rims with 16 to 18 spokes gave a 7% benefit at 25 mph, which surprisingly bettered the 4% advantage of a single rear or set of disc wheels and equaled the benefit of a specially designed aerodynamic bicycle.[200]

Conditioning

Conditioning, or training, improves performance in several ways. It increases maximum energy output (important for short events such as sprints) as well as increasing the muscle's efficiency for any given level of exertion (reflected in improved results for longer-duration events).

Training effects are specific for the muscle groups being exercised (activity or sport specific) as well as improving the cardiovascular system (benefiting all aerobic activities).

Improvements in performance are the result of :
(1) an increase in the number and size of muscle mitochondria,
(2) an increase in the activity of metabolic enzymes in the muscle cell,
(3) an increase in the number of capillaries that supply blood to the muscle, and
(4) an increase in cardiac output.

Although some of these changes begin within days of starting a training program, and most positive effects are seen within a few months, there is evidence that training will continue to produce improvements after many years. One study suggested that regular training can lead to a conversion from Type II to the more efficient Type I muscle fibers, and that these changes continued through 5 years of regular exercise. [201]

Although athletic performance is the ultimate yardstick of training improvement, the effects of conditioning can be measured in several other ways. First, the percentage of Calories derived from fat metabolism at any given activity level or percentage of V_{O2max} (Fig. 1.2) is increased. [2, 27] This promotes glycogen sparing and increases the duration of activity to exhaustion for any level of exertion.

Second, V_{O2max} or maximum possible energy production from glucose is increased. This means that at maximal or near-maximal performance, more energy will be supplied from efficient aerobic metabolism than from inefficient anaerobic metabolism.

Third, there is a shift in the blood lactate threshold (LT) so that less lactic acid accumulates for any specified level of energy output. This reflects both a decrease in production (i.e., a shift toward more efficient aerobic glucose metabolism) and a more rapid clearance of the lactic acid produced. As lactic acid has a negative effect on muscle contractile proteins, this shift in the LT minimizes deterioration in muscle performance.

The benefit of these training changes is to allow a well-trained individual to perform at any given level of activity (a certain cycling speed for example) for a longer time before his or her glycogen reserves are depleted (i.e., before the bonk occurs) or to maintain more glycogen reserves for a sprint at the end of the race than a less-trained competitor.

Cross Training

A popular myth is that one can cross train for aerobic events. For example, a runner could cycle in the summer and then resume running in the fall with little change in performance.

While the concept of cross training is valid for the recreational athlete attempting to maintain a general level of cardiovascular conditioning, it is not an option for the competitive athlete. As noted above, most of the benefits of conditioning are at the musculo-skeletal level and are specific for the muscle groups being used.

Many studies of triathletes, for example, have consistently demonstrated that cycling does not improve running performance, running slightly improves cycling performance and that swimming has no effect whatsoever on the other events, or vice versa. [203, 204, 205]

Cycling and Weight Control

Aerobic exercise can play an important role in a weight-control program. Physical activity has a positive effect on weight loss through appetite suppression, increased energy expenditure, and the maintenance of lean muscle tissue at the expense of fat. The basic premise of all weight-control programs is that the number of Calories being expended by the body should be greater than the number of Calories consumed, resulting in an overall net deficit. This deficit is covered by Calories derived from the body's fat reserves, resulting in weight loss. It has been shown that exercise is a more effective means of stabilizing weight after weight loss than continued Calorie restriction.[206]

One interesting observation in this area was the unavoidable weight loss that occurs in some competitive athletes no matter how many Calories they attempted to eat. When examined closely, this was found to be a result of the Calories expended being more than the number eaten. This was most pronounced in competitive swimmers. As a group, they would train long hours, were unable to eat while swimming, and had too few waking hours left to replace the Calories (as many as 7,000 Calories with only 6 or 7 non-exercise waking hours). Because cyclists can eat while riding, this is less of a problem for this sport.[4]

One unconfirmed study suggested that there was an advantage to cycling over other activities in a weight-loss program. The dieters were divided into three exercise groups—swimmers, walkers, and cyclists. For an equivalent exercise level, the cyclists lost the most weight.[19] It will be interesting to see if these results can be duplicated by other researchers.

Many dieters claim that vigorous activity actually increases their appetite, and several early population studies appeared to support the idea that appetite was regulated by exercise in such a way as to maintain a constant body weight. This implied that any weight-loss benefits of exercise would be limited unless the individual had extreme self-control. However, recent, more carefully controlled studies of overweight individuals have proven that additional physical activity does not stimulate a proportionate increase in appetite and is helpful in achieving a net negative caloric balance and weight loss.

An additional benefit of vigorous exercise is the suppression of appetite that occurs immediately afterward and lasts for several hours. This short-term effect can be used as an appetite-control strategy by planning an exercise period immediately prior to the major meal of the day.

Cycling, or any other exercise program, increases an individual's caloric expenditures in several ways. First, and most significant, is the immediate energy requirement of the working muscles to move bicycle and rider against the resistance of the air and gravity. The number of Calories consumed is a function of the weight of the bicycle and its rider, the speed at which they are moving, and the duration of the ride. An additional, indirect effect is that individuals in an exercise program report an increased vigor and sense of wellbeing, often changing other aspects of their daily routine to include more physical activity—for example, routinely walking up a flight of stairs instead of taking the elevator.

Exercise also has a beneficial effect on the basal metabolic rate, or BMR (the number of Calories utilized when the body is at rest to maintain the basic life processes). Recent studies have demonstrated that a regular exercise program not only prevents the usual slowing of the basal rate associated with dietary restriction (a natural adaptive response to starvation), but have also hinted at an increase in the BMR compared to that on a normal diet without exercise. These effects on the BMR are associated with all aerobic conditioning activity and can be maintained with 30–40 minutes of vigorous exercise 3 or 4 times a week.

A final benefit of physical activity relates to the protection of muscle mass during periods of caloric restriction and weight loss. This results in the preferential loss of body fat and preservation of muscle when weight loss occurs.

Both as a measure of their efficiency as energy sources, and as a measure of their respective impact on a weight-control program, Table 2.1 compares the number of Calories supplied to the body by carbohydrates, fats, and protein.

Although the bottom line of any cycling weight-control program will be read from the bathroom scale, a rough estimate of

weight change is possible using the information in Table 2.2 and
Table 2.3.

Table 2.1 Energy contents of carbohydrates, fats, and proteins

Food type	Energy content Cal/g	(kJ/g)
carbohydrates (both starch and sugars)	4.1	(17.2)
fats (both dietary fat and body fat)	9.3	(38.9)
protein	4.1	(17.2)

Table 2.2 Cycling and weight control

C_i = Calorie intake per 24 hrs. = ... Cal

C_b = basal metabolic rate per 24 hrs.
(men: weight in lbs × .45 × 24)
(women: weight in lbs × .45 × 24) = ... Cal

C_e = Calories expended by cycling
Table 2.3 (miles ridden × Cal/mile) = ... Cal

C_a = Adjustment for BMR in Table 2.3
(hrs. of exercise × 50 cal/hr.) = ... Cal

C_n = net calorie gain or loss per 24 hrs.
$C_i - C_b - C_e + C_a =$ . . . . Cal

Weight gain or loss in pounds per 24 hrs.
$C_n \div 3,500 =$ . . . . . lbs

Table 2.3 Caloric expenditure when cycling

Riding speed		Calories expended			
m.p.h.	(km/h)	Cal/mile	(Cal/km)	Cal/hr	(Cal/min)
5	(8.0)	7.4	(4.6)	87	(1.5)
6	(9.6)	8.3	(5.2)	100	(1.7)
7	(11.2)	9.3	(5.8)	115	(1.9)
8	(12.8)	10.5	(6.6)	134	(2.2)
9	(14.4)	11.9	(7.4)	157	(2.6)
10	(16.0)	13.4	(8.4)	184	(3.1)
11	(17.6)	15.1	(9.4)	216	(3.6)
12	(19.2)	16.9	(10.6)	253	(4.2)
13	(20.8)	18.9	(11.8)	296	(4.9)
14	(22.4)	21.1	(13.2)	345	(5.7)
15	(24.0)	23.4	(14.6)	401	(6.7)
16	(25.6)	25.8	(16.2)	463	(7.7)
17	(27.2)	28.5	(17.8)	534	(8.9)
18	(28.8)	31.3	(19.5)	613	(10.2)
19	(30.4)	34.2	(21.4)	700	(11.7)
20	(32.0)	37.3	(23.3)	797	(13.3)
21	(33.6)	40.6	(25.4)	903	(15.0)
22	(35.2)	44.0	(27.5)	1019	(17.0)
23	(36.7)	47.6	(29.8)	1146	(19.1)
24	(38.4)	51.4	(32.1)	1283	(21.4)
25	(40.0)	55.3	(34.6)	1433	(23.9)
26	(41.6)	59.4	(37.1)	1594	(26.6)
27	(43.2)	63.6	(39.8)	1767	(29.5)
28	(44.8)	68.0	(42.5)	1954	(32.6)
29	(46.4)	72.5	(45.3)	2154	(35.9)
30	(48.0)	77.2	(48.2)	2365	(39.4)

Remarks:
Values are based on the following assumptions:
1. 75-kg rider with 10-kg bicycle;
2. 25% efficiency of the human "machine";
3. basal metabolism of 50 Cal/hr.
For estimation purposes, values are sufficiently accurate for all cyclists.

CHAPTER 3

Nutrition Theory

Now that we have covered the basic physiology of digestion and the energy requirements of cycling, let's use this information to develop a practical nutrition program that will maximize our performance and enjoyment of the sport.

General Background

The typical American diet provides 46% of the Calories as carbohydrates (16% from free sugars and 30% from complex carbohydrates), 42% from fats, and 12% from protein. There has been a gradual change over the the last 50 years, with an increase in fats from 32% to 42%, at the expense of complex carbohydrates, which have declined from 40% to 30%.[46]

Carbohydrates (fruits, vegetables, and grains) are the primary source of energy for the human power plant. By providing this fuel, they spare stored fats and, more importantly, cellular proteins that would otherwise be broken down and metabolized for their energy content. Beyond their value as an energy source, carbohydrates are not essential for any specific metabolic function.

Recently there has been increased interest in the type of carbohydrates in the diet, comparing the relative effects of simple carbohydrates, such as refined sugar, to those of complex carbohydrates (starches). Increasingly, evidence supports both a health and sports performance advantage of complex carbohydrates. They are absorbed more slowly, require less insulin for their metabolism and, as a result, produce a more even and constant blood sugar level.

Fats are another energy source but differ from carbohydrates in providing essential building blocks for the cellular machinery. That is, they cannot be synthesized or produced by the body and must be included in the diet. These essential fats include certain fatty acids (linoleic acid), as well as cholesterol and phospholipids. It has been estimated that these essential requirements would be met with a diet containing only 15–25 grams of fat

(135–225 Calories, or about 10% of our total daily caloric needs), while additional fat Calories are used only for their energy value.

Studies of the various groups of nonessential dietary fats have repeatedly demonstrated the harmful effects of saturated animal fats as opposed to the benefits of unsaturated vegetable fats and certain fatty acids found in fish oils (eicosapentaenoic acid). These findings, coupled with the evidence that a diet which is high in fat contributes to obesity and heart disease, have resulted in strong recommendations to cut the percentage of our daily Calories provided by fats and to use "good" fats in food preparation whenever possible. There are limits to these reductions, however, as fat content is important to the texture and taste appeal of food.

Proteins are the third major constituent of our diet. While fats and carbohydrates are used as energy sources for our daily activities, protein provides the basic building blocks for cell growth and repair. As with fats, there are certain essential amino acids (the building blocks of proteins) which cannot be produced by the body and are mandatory dietary requirements. However, once these needs have been met there is no evidence that additional protein is helpful, even to the vigorous athlete. The additional dietary protein required for the muscle growth stimulated by conditioning is quite small when compared to the normal daily intake, and there is no evidence that a high-protein diet will speed up or force this muscle development. In fact, there is some evidence that a routinely high-protein diet may be harmful to the kidneys.

Ongoing interest and research into the health effects of the American diet will undoubtedly result in further changes. The evidence suggests that this will include an overall reduction in fat content, emphasizing the benefits of certain types of fats, with a corresponding increase in the carbohydrate content to make up the Calorie deficit.

Based on the physiology reviewed in Chapter 1, it is easy to identify carbohydrates as the optimum energy food for all athletic activities. They are easily digested and absorbed, and are also the most readily metabolized to ATP. Fats have the disadvantage of slowing gastric emptying and absorption, while proteins have a very complex metabolism that limits their availability as an energy source.

During exercise, certain carbohydrate stores are used preferentially to meet the energy needs of the muscle cell. The glucose stored in the muscle fibers as glycogen is used first. Once the muscle glycogen has been depleted, the blood becomes the most important glucose source. As blood glucose (blood sugar) is used, it is replaced by glycogen from the liver. Any glucose absorbed from the digestive tract helps to conserve the liver glycogen. When the liver glycogen is depleted, the muscle cell is dependent on either absorbed glucose or fat metabolism to meet its energy needs. If there is no glucose available from digestion, hypoglycemia and fatigue occur.[11, 35] The athlete has now "hit the wall."

Pre-Exercise Diet

The body's glycogen stores on a normal diet (365 grams, or 1,500 Calories) will support several hours of submaximal cycling before complete depletion and fatigue occur. Although this is adequate for the average recreational cyclist and for competitive events lasting less than one hour, the endurance rider or racer participating in longer events will benefit from pre-exercise carbohydrate loading to maximize muscle glycogen reserves.

The amount of glycogen stored in the muscles is directly related to the carbohydrate content of the diet. After 3 days on a high-carbohydrate diet (providing at least 70% of the total dietary Calories in the form of carbohydrate), total muscle glycogen stores are significantly greater than after a standard diet. When muscle glycogen is depleted by vigorous exercise immediately before beginning a high-carbohydrate diet, this difference is accentuated.

A standard carbohydrate loading program is started 6 days prior to the anticipated competitive event. A vigorous daily workout of 1–2 hours each of the first 3 days depletes the muscles' glycogen reserves. During this period, the athlete stays on a low-carbohydrate diet (a maximum of 10% of total Calories from carbohydrates) to maximize the depletion effects of exercise. This is followed by 3 days of a carbohydrate-rich diet with only light exercise to maintain muscle flexibility. During these final 3 days, the cyclist should eat at least 600 grams of carbohydrate per 24 hours.

The last carbohydrates are consumed 4–6 hours prior to the event.[28, 40]

Some disadvantages of carbohydrate loading include the difficulty of maintaining the initial low-carbohydrate diet, problems with weight gain during the high-carbohydrate and low-exercise portion of the program, and complaints of muscle heaviness and stiffness thought to result from the excess glycogen and associated water present in the muscle fibers.

The amount of water retention is not insignificant. For each gram of carbohydrate stored, 3 grams of water are stored as well. This equals a 2–7 pound weight gain from water alone.[52] This water retention may have a positive effect in that, as glycogen is utilized during exercise, the water released will cut down fluid replacement needs. Although there have been additional concerns about EKG (cardiac) changes due to glycogen loading of the heart muscle, as well as possible long-term harmful effects, these have not been substantiated.[3]

Even though muscle glycogen is predictably increased with this program, it is not clear that performance is enhanced beyond a 3-day high-carbohydrate diet alone, i.e., without the initial depletion phase.[40] One study indicated that trained endurance athletes achieved the maximum possible muscle glycogen stores with rest and a high-carbohydrate diet alone.[6] Considering the potential problems and questionable benefit of a full 6-day program, most athletic trainers are currently recommending 3 days of high carbohydrate intake immediately prior to the event and are eliminating the depletion phase.

There is a consensus on the importance of the pre-race meal. While it may take up to 3 days to replace or maximize muscle glycogen, liver glycogen is much more readily modified by diet. The pre-race meal may "top off" these liver stores. A recent study that demonstrated a 15% increase in endurance performance with a 300-gram solid carbohydrate meal taken 4 hours before exercise credited this improvement to prolonged digestion with continued glucose absorption well into the exercise period. [207]

Although carbohydrates are beneficial in a pre-exercise program, there is one critical period during which their intake should be limited—the several hours immediately prior to exercise. With the insulin surge that follows the absorption of carbohydrates, and the additive effect of exercise to facilitate the movement of glucose into the cell, there is the possibility of hypoglycemia and the risk of poor performance as a result. Thus it is currently recommended that only complex carbohydrates—not simple sugars—be eaten, and then at least several hours before exercise.

A second issue in the immediate pre-event phase is the tendency of nervousness to delay gastric emptying. To avoid the stomach distention that can develop, any nutrition should be taken at least 3 hours before the event, and should be as low in fat as possible.

The best strategy appears to be a low-fat, 300-gram carbohydrate meal 4 hours before the event, and a 45-gram confectionery bar high in simple and complex carbohydrates 5 minutes before. [6, 207]

There has been very little work on the fat and protein requirements in the pre-exercise period, and no suggestion that either is of any benefit. A common misconception already mentioned is that an increase in dietary protein will force muscle development. The only stimulus for muscle growth is resistive training, or conditioning. A normal balanced diet provides more than enough protein to support the maximum achievable muscle-mass increase of one pound per week. In fact, increasing dietary protein may be counterproductive if protein Calories replace carbohydrate in the 3-day pre-exercise period. The same is true for fats, which are notorious for their appetite-suppressant effect. Although some trainers have suggested that fats in the immediate pre-exercise meal are helpful, it has been clearly demonstrated that the consumption of easily digested fat in the form of medium-chain triglycerides was no better than placebo in improving performance. [207]

Some final words of caution: avoid any major changes in diet during the pre-competition period. The above suggestions need to be customized for your own digestive and metabolic functions. Any advantage of carbohydrate loading, or shifting the make-up of your diet, can be more than offset by the GI distress or indigestion brought on by new foods or food combinations. As in all things, moderation is important, and a balanced diet with an emphasis on carbohydrates appears to offer the maximum benefits during this period.

Exercise

Early in the exercise period, almost all the glucose fuel for the muscle cell comes from muscle glycogen. As this muscle glycogen is steadily depleted, the percentage of energy supplied from blood glucose steadily increases until it reaches 100% in the third and fourth hour.[11, 35] Initially, the blood sugar level is maintained by the breakdown and release of liver glycogen. However, at 3 to 4 hours it is estimated that 75% of the glucose metabolized is from oral intake and 25% is from either liver glycogen or gluco-neogenesis (i.e., glucose formed as an intermediate step in fat or protein metabolism).[10]

This relationship between muscle, liver, and blood glucose explains the performance-enhancing effect of oral carbohydrate feedings for exercise lasting more than one hour. In fact, one study suggested that after only one hour of exercise, blood sugar was already supplying 75%–90% of the carbohydrate needed for metabolism by the muscles.[6] If oral caloric supplements are started early in the ride, they conserve muscle and liver glycogen and delay the time at which complete depletion (fatigue) occurs.[11, 209] Any carbohydrates taken in after liver glycogen may have been exhausted provide a noticeable immediate energy boost.

It should be remembered that fats in the form of FFA also supply energy for the active muscle. The fact that fat metabolism provides a greater percentage of the total Calories expended at lower V_{O2} presents another option to protect the body's glycogen reserves. Indeed, "going out fast" at more than 70% of V_{O2max} is very inefficient in terms of glycogen use, with almost all the expended Calories coming from muscle and liver glycogen. The more prudent cyclist marshals his or her resources at 50%–70% V_{O2max}, which spares both muscle and liver glycogen by increasing the energy Calories from FFA metabolism.[6]

The type of sugar eaten, i.e., glucose versus fructose, does not appear to be a factor one way or another, but the form of the supplement does.[6, 30] One study compared equal caloric feedings of liquid and solid carbohydrates and demonstrated that although maximum pace, heart rate, and total energy expenditure were the same, the riders eating the more solid carbohydrate were able to sustain a longer sprint to exhaustion at the end of the ride.[9] It can be speculated that this was due to a more sustained release of glucose energy from the additional time needed to digest and absorb the solid carbohydrate.[1]

This suggests that solid carbohydrates are preferable early in the ride. On the other hand, when a quick energy boost is needed (that is, after all glycogen reserves have been exhausted), it is logical that a liquid glucose drink would be optimal. This minimizes a delay in stomach emptying and absorption time, although frequent drinks will be required to maintain these benefits.

Recently glucose polymers, complex molecules made up of individual glucose molecules, have been developed and marketed both as a powder and as ready-mixed sports drinks. These appear to combine the beneficial characteristics of being readily absorbed due to their liquid form and of providing the prolonged benefits of more slowly digested and absorbed complex carbohydrates.[24]

Once again, there has been little work on the effects of fats and protein eaten during the exercise period. Fats improve the taste of snacks and may be helpful in counteracting the natural depression of appetite that occurs with exercise, but delays in stomach emptying may lead to nausea if taken in large amounts. The same is true for proteins, though to a lesser degree.

In 1984, White and his associates analyzed the diet of an ultra-distance cyclist during a 24-hour event.[45] They found that the percentage of total energy derived from proteins (10%) and fats (30%) decreased, with a marked shift toward carbohydrates (60%). This compares with the normal pattern of 15% protein, 40% fat, and 45% carbohydrate. There was also an increase in the intake of liquids, with semisolid (36%) and liquid foods (30%) providing more than half the Calories. This shift appeared to result from the increased fluid needs of exercise as well as from the decreased sensation of abdominal fullness due to the improved gastric emptying and absorption of liquids. Even with these changes, and a strong emphasis on maintaining a good intake during the ride, it was still possible to supply only a little more than half (54%) of the total estimated energy requirements of the event (19,755 Calories).

Post-Exercise Diet

The most common mistake in exercise nutrition is the failure to appreciate the importance of the post-exercise diet. Most athletes feel that after a long training ride or competitive event the only diet issue is when to begin carbohydrate loading for the next session. There are two important benefits of a good post-exercise regimen, and once again both the selection of carbohydrates as the preferred food and the timing of replacement play key roles.

Muscle glycogen depletion is felt to play a role in the stiffness that follows strenuous exercise. It appears that one benefit of vigorous carbohydrate repletion is to minimize this "day-after effect" of a training ride or competitive event. A second issue is the fact that failure to completely replace the muscle glycogen stores depleted by a regular vigorous training program may contribute to the stale feeling that occurs after several consecutive days of exercise. Blunting both of these results of glycogen depletion would be helpful in meeting training goals.

Liver glycogen is restored quickly and easily if a high-carbohydrate diet is followed. On the other hand, complete muscle glycogen replacement requires 48 hours, although the majority of the replacement is accomplished in the first 24 hours.[6, 8] As in pre-event carbohydrate loading, a daily intake of 600 grams of carbohydrate achieves optimal results, and it appears that complex carbohydrates (starches) are superior to free glucose in speedily completing the process.[6, 49]

During the hours immediately following vigorous exercise, glycogen synthesis in the muscles proceeds at a rate three times that 6 to 12 hours later, when adequate glucose is available.[25] A 100-gram liquid carbohydrate drink immediately after exercise, repeated again 2 hours later, maximized this effect.[208] The athlete who is in a multiday competitive event or trains daily will use this strategy to his or her advantage to maximize reloading muscle glycogen stores for the next day's activity.

Although some muscle breakdown occurs with all vigorous exercise, the normal American diet contains more than enough protein to provide the raw materials for any repairs necessary in the post-exercise period.

Water

Water is not a source of nutrition, yet adequate hydration is at least as important to good athletic performance as the type and form of food eaten. Total body fluid losses during exercise result in a decrease in both plasma volume (the fluid circulating within the blood vessels) and muscle water. As this fluid loss progresses, physical performance deteriorates.

The degree of dehydration determines the effect on physiologic function and athletic performance. A loss of 2% of body weight from dehydration will impair heat regulation, but not the function of the muscle cells themselves. However, at a 3% deficit, the endurance time for muscle contraction is reduced and at 4% this effect on endurance can translate into a 5%–10% drop in performance. At 6% severe medical complications can result. Because both sweat production and insensible loss through the lungs can each exceed 2 quarts per hour a fluid deficit can develop quite quickly. Maintaining plasma volume is one of the hidden keys to optimal physical performance.

A practical assessment of the importance of dehydration on cycling performance was undertaken by White and Ford in 1983.[44] In this study, seven elite cycling endurance performers completed a 103-km course over a 2½-hour period at an average speed of 41.9 km/h (26 mph). They found that:

1. body-weight losses averaged 3.25%;

2. relatively low volumes of fluid were ingested during the race;

3. little or no fluid intake occurred in two competitors who retired early with symptoms of heat distress.

The results indicated that even medium-distance road racing produced significant body-weight (fluid) loss. Even more significant was the finding that most of the cyclists involved in the study were unaware of the importance of fluid intake in minimizing the harmful effects of dehydration on performance.

In a second study, an experimental protocol was designed using a windload simulator. Work loads were structured to require approximately 67% of each subject's previously determined maximum aerobic performance (V_{O2max}). This resulted in an average weight loss of 1.9% at 1 hour and 3.6% at 2 hours if no fluids were ingested. Physiologic measurements were made with no fluid replacement, with complete replacement using water, and with replacement using an electrolyte drink. Without replacement, there was increasing work intolerance, as indicated by an increase in heart rate and systolic blood pressure. With ongoing replacement, this effect was minimized and there was a more rapid return to the pre-exercise baseline during the recovery period. Aside from a taste preference, there was no apparent benefit with the electrolyte drink over water alone during the 2-hour trial. However, the fact that relatively large fluid volumes needed to be replaced (2,300 ml) suggests that palatability and gastric tolerance are important considerations in the selection of replacement fluids.

The most outstanding finding was how rapidly serious fluid deficiencies could occur with minimal awareness on the part of the athlete. It again points out that the sensation of thirst lags well behind the body's needs, and that a successful fluid replacement program needs to begin at the same time as the ride.[44]

Sports Drinks

Carbohydrate drinks, so-called sports drinks, are important if a strenuous ride of more than 2 hours is planned. The body's glycogen will support vigorous exercise for approximately 2 hours before depletion and fatigue occur. Any carbohydrate ingested during this period will spare these glycogen reserves. Although this does not increase maximum performance levels, it will prolong the duration of exercise before exhaustion occurs. To put this into perspective, a 10% glucose solution, equivalent to a regular cola or similar soft drink, taken at a quart per hour would provide 260 Calories. A 165-lb cyclist riding at 15 mph burns 400 Calories/hr; at 20 mph, 800 Calories/hr are required (see Table 2.3). Thus this replacement would give a 25%–50% increase in endurance. These drinks are also a convenient way to supplement the training diet during the 4-hour post-exercise replacement interval.

While exercise physiologists agree that carbohydrate replacement is of benefit in prolonged exercise, there is considerable debate on the merits of carbohydrate polymers versus simple sugars (glucose). Neither David Lamb, at Ohio State's Human Performance Laboratory, nor Mark Davis, at the University of South Carolina, have been able to demonstrate any advantage to glucose polymers over simple sugars in enhancing performance.[51] Likewise, a study by Quaker Oats found no difference in the enhancement of long-distance cycling performance when a 6%

sucrose/glucose solution was compared to a 7% glucose polymer/fructose drink.[51]

Although they appear to be physiologically equivalent when equal Calories are provided, the advantage of polymers is tghat they are not as sweet as simple sugar drinks, because sweet tasting drinks discourage fluid replacement,.

Although most research has analyzed solutions with a sugar concentration of 6%–8%, there is some suggestive work that concentrations of up to 20%–25% may be well tolerated by athletes who have used them regularly in training. This is particularly important for ultra-endurance athletes who expend thousands of Calories per day and, as a result, have great difficulty meeting their energy replacement requirements.

Drugs and Vitamins

Once competitive cyclists understand and master the basics of nutrition, they often seek to further enhance their performance with supplements. Some, such as ephedrine, are banned in sanctioned competitive events and will not be discussed further.

The use of dietary supplements to enhance performance can be traced back at least as far as the Romans, who drank lion's blood to improve their strength and courage. Today's additives, mainly amino acids and vitamins, are often used with little more proof of benefit than was available to the Romans. In addition to the lack of any controlled scientific studies to support their benefits, the potential side effects as well as the high cost of these supplements need to be considered.

Occasionally articles will appear touting the benefits of alcohol as an energy source for sports activities. Although alcohol contains 7 Cal/gram and is rapidly absorbed from the intestinal tract, its actual negative effects outweigh any theoretical positive ones. It is a diuretic, contributing to dehydration; it slows down glucose production and release from the liver; and it disturbs motor skills, including the balance and coordination essential for proper bike handling. The sum total is a definite and surprisingly large negative influence on performance.

Vitamins are often held up as a safe and effective way of improving performance. Although they are frequently recommended by coaches and used by competitive athletes, there is no evidence that any athlete on a balanced diet improves his or her performance with vitamin supplements. In addition, there is good evidence that mega-vitamin programs can be harmful. This is particularly true with the fat-soluble vitamins (A, E, D, and K), which can accumulate in the body and reach toxic levels. But even with the use of water-soluble vitamins (B-complex and C), any excess of which is excreted in the urine, there have been reports of harmful side effects at mega-doses (usually 10 to 100 times the recommended daily requirements). If there is a concern about how well-balanced your diet is, there is no harm (other than to your wallet) in using a simple over-the-counter multiple vitamin once a day "just to be safe."

Amino acids are the building blocks of proteins and are present in all foods. As with vitamins, a balanced diet should provide more than enough of the essential amino acids, and there is no proof (with the possible exception of L-carnitine) that the available supplements enhance performance. The amino acids sold in the health food store for $20–$30 per bottle have no proven advantage over a glass of milk and a peanut butter sandwich, and don't have nearly the taste appeal. In addition, too much protein in the diet has a diuretic effect that increases the risk of dehydration; excessive protein can also cause diarrhea and abdominal bloating and, by placing an additional burden on the kidneys, may lead to chronic renal damage. Because an increase in carbohydrates, particularly during training, has a protein-sparing effect, there is another alternative—adding jelly to the peanut butter sandwich!

Of the popular supplements, vitamin B_{15} (also known as D_{15} or pangamic acid), octacosanol, trimethylglycine, gamma-oryzanol, and inosine are of unproven benefit. L-carnitine, sodium bicarbonate, phosphate, and caffeine may be of some use in certain situations.

L-carnitine is the only amino acid that has been studied in conditioned athletes and has been suggested to improve performance. In an Italian study it was found to promote glycogen sparing (through increased utilization of fatty acids), allowing a longer ride to exhaustion. In addition, there was the hint that conditioned athletes could also raise their V_{O2max}.[34] However, these results have not been confirmed by other investigators, and the potential side effects of this agent have not been completely explored.

Sodium bicarbonate is another substance that has been studied in a controlled manner and has been demonstrated to improve performance. It is available in the form of baking soda or Alka-Seltzer, and presumably works by neutralizing the lactic acid that builds up in the muscles during exercise. The blood's natural buffering capacity provides this buffering during sustained exercise, but bicarbonate appears to help during short sprints, when lactic acid accumulates more quickly. In a study at Iowa State University, cyclists improved their sprinting ability significantly by taking 2 tablespoons of baking soda just prior to the event. However, side effects such as diarrhea and stomach upset were common, and it appears to be of use only in short races such as the 4,000 meter pursuit.[9, 34]

A blood phosphate compound, 2, 3 diphosphoglycerate (DPG), binds with hemoglobin to facilitate the release of oxygen at the level of the muscle capillaries. As phosphate is a building block of DPG, it seemed reasonable to consider that oral phosphate might be of benefit to athletic performance. In a single study, phosphate in the form of sodium phosphate taken in a dose of 600 mg six times a day for 3 days increased V_{O2max} by 10% and cycling performance by 20%.[210] It will be interesting to see if this startling study can be duplicated.

Drugs that stimulate muscle growth, such as anabolic steroids, human growth hormone, the drug periactin, and the herb ginseng, have all been used to improve performance. However, their side effects present a significant health hazard to the user. Only growth hormone is currently being investigated for its potential role in preventing the muscle changes that occur with aging. However, these same changes can also be offset with a regular exercise program, avoiding the potential side effects.

Caffeine

No discussion of performance enhancers would be complete without mentioning caffeine. During prolonged (endurance) exercise, the onset of fatigue correlates closely with the depletion of muscle glycogen stores and is delayed if muscle glycogen is spared. The metabolism of free fatty acids as an alternative energy source results in a decreased use of muscle glycogen during exercise. Caffeine does increase blood FFA, and in one study produced a 50% increase peaking at 3 to 4 hours.[49] This effect on FFA was seen after a dose of 5 mg/kg of body weight, which is the equivalent of 2 cups of coffee (300 mg caffeine) for a 70-kg person.[36]

A second possibility is that caffeine works on the central nervous system as a general stimulant and suppresses pain from the lactate buildup during anaerobic exercise.[9]

There are also negative effects to caffeine. One is the diuretic effect, which leads to frequent urination and results in a body-fluid deficit and dehydration. Others are an increased heart rate and anxiety. But by far the biggest negative is that caffeine in high concentrations is considered a drug and is banned by the U.S. Olympic Committee.

Controversy continues over the practical benefits of caffeine. The original study at Ball State University demonstrated a 20% increase in endurance performance after the equivalent of 3 cups of coffee or 6 caffeinated colas. Further studies have been less convincing. In addition, physiologists believe that caffeine's effects may be negated on race day because of high adrenaline levels. Nonetheless, the consensus of endurance athletes is that caffeine can be useful if used correctly. This includes a period of abstinence for several weeks before the race, because habitual use induces tolerance.[34]

To put additives in their proper perspective, it should be noted that 35% of all subjects have a positive response to any pill, including those without an active ingredient—the placebo response. It is possible that this psychological lift is the major benefit of most performance enhancers. Any improvement in the few controlled studies done thus far has been small, a few percent at most, and would be of benefit only to the competitive athlete already on an optimum training and nutritional program. The average recreational cyclist, on the other hand, has little if anything to gain from this group of substances.

Minerals, Trace Elements

Minerals are chemical elements found in the body either in their elemental form or complexed with organic molecules. Like vitamins, they are essential for normal cell functioning. The two most prevalent minerals, calcium and phosphorous, are major components of bone, while sodium and potassium are found in all tissue fluids, both within and around the cells. Magnesium, chloride, sulfur, and zinc are other minerals that play a key role in cell function. The trace elements iron, manganese, copper, and iodine are found in much smaller quantities, but play essential roles as catalysts in basic cellular chemical processes.

These minerals, found in all foods, are kept in balance through regulation of both absorption and excretion. As a result of this close control, they are easily provided by a balanced diet. With the increase in Calories required to meet training needs, the athlete enjoys the additional protection of an increased mineral intake and, as a result, mineral deficiencies are extremely rare, even on unusual training diets. Only calcium and iron may be required by some athletes in increased amounts. Because of toxic side effects when taken in large amounts, minerals as a group are not recommended as routine dietary supplements.

This is also true for sodium chloride, or table salt. Over a 24-hour period, the athlete's standard training diet replaces two to three times the normal salt losses. Only under extreme environmental conditions of high temperature or high humidity is a salt supplement needed. An exception may be the cyclist who has not trained for an event and can lose excessive amounts of salt in perspiration.[36, 49, 52] Although exercise cramps were once thought to be a result of salt deficiency, it now appears that they are a heat cramp related to dehydration and a decreased blood flow to the muscles.[30]

Calcium metabolism in the athlete is still not completely understood. The question of an increased calcium requirement is linked to concerns about osteoporosis in women athletes who, because of the intensity of their training, have become amenorrheic. The hormonal changes that occur with amenorrhea affect bone formation and are thought to be the cause of osteoporosis. Recent evidence has suggested that the positive effects of exercise on bone formation may counteract and cancel out this bone loss. At this time, there is no consensus on the need for calcium supplements, and the controversy is mentioned here for completeness only.

Iron, on the other hand, has been studied extensively in athletes. A deficiency state does occur and has a negative effect on performance. Again, this is more of a problem for the woman athlete, because of the additional iron needed to replace menstrual blood loss. When the U.S. Olympic team was studied, it was found that 20%–30% of the female athletes did not get adequate iron from their diet alone.[22] As iron can be toxic, any question of a deficiency state is best resolved by a screening blood count and serum iron or ferritin assay before resorting to supplements.

Fiber

Dietary fiber has received considerable attention during the last few years. Fiber is a general term for the non-digestible carbohydrate in the diet and refers mainly to the cellulose, lignin, and pectin found in fruits, grains, and vegetables.

Its major function is to provide bulk in the diet to aid in regular elimination. There is evidence that population groups with a traditionally low-fiber diet also have an increased incidence of diverticulosis, cardiovascular disease, colon cancer, and diabetes. The difficulty with these studies is that the ethnic groups that eat a low-fiber diet also have a higher percentage of their total dietary Calories provided by fats and refined sugars. Therefore, it may be the excess fats, for example, rather than the lack of fiber that is the culprit.

Currently there is no recommended minimum for dietary fiber and no special requirements for cyclists or other athletes. On the other hand, there is evidence that too much fiber may bind minerals such as zinc in the intestinal tract, resulting in poor absorption. The most reasonable approach seems to be a well-balanced diet with enough fruits, grains, and vegetables to maintain regular bowel function.

Pritikin Diet

Although most active cyclists tend to eat a high-carbohydrate diet, the concept is pushed to the limit by the Pritikin diet.[38] This diet, or rather eating program, stresses a high intake of complex carbohydrates (75%–80% of total Calories) and a marked reduction in fat and protein (each contributing 10%).

In his writings, Pritikin relates numerous testimonials from triathletes and other endurance athletes to support his claims of improved athletic performance. His concept, which amounts to continuous carbohydrate loading, is well presented and appears to be supported in practice. Aside from the somewhat monotonous nature of the meal plans, this regimen may be a reasonable consideration, both for the athlete in training and for those who feel a need to modify the high-fat Western diet. Whether or not it actually improves performance is as yet unresolved.

Psychological Effects of Foods

A common question is, "do the foods we eat have an effect on our mood or attitude?" When looked at critically in the trained athlete, the only association was an increase in depression scores on standardized psychologic profiles when there was a deficit in caloric replacement needs in the training diet. This was felt to be a normal response to the chronic fatigue that occurs in this situation, particularly in the trained athlete who expects the best from him or herself at all times.

Beyond this, any psychological effects are probably nonspecific and related either to the feeling of well-being that follows eating a meal or the placebo effect of a favorite food.

CHAPTER 4

Nutrition for the Recreational Cyclist

The next two chapters will use the basic physiology and nutritional concepts presented thus far to develop nutritional programs for cyclists of all abilities. This chapter will analyze the needs of the recreational rider, while the next will focus on the competitive or elite cyclist.

The Casual and Commuter Cyclist

The casual or commuter cyclist will ride for 1 or 2 hours daily at 50%–60% of his or her V_{O2max}. The goal is a comfortable ride with adequate energy for the remainder of the day.

There is no specific benefit to a training diet for this group, but adherence to a balanced diet with 60%–70% of total Calories from carbohydrates is suggested.

Nutrition on the go. Grabbing a snack from the pouch is usually safe only while riding at a relaxed pace.

Likewise the pre-ride period is quite flexible. Even with a 4-hour fast there will be adequate glycogen stores to ride 2 hours at this cycling speed. However, a high-carbohydrate breakfast, eaten at least an hour before the ride, will spare these glycogen stores and lessen the chance of "running out of gas" later in the day.

During the ride, a water bottle of water (20 ounces) per hour should eliminate any concerns about dehydration. A carbo-hydrate supplement is optional and, again, will help preserve body glycogen stores for use later in the day.

Post-ride nutrition should include a high-carbohydrate snack or meal, especially if there was not a pre-ride meal or glucose sup-plementation during the ride itself. If glycogen reserves have been depleted, there is a risk of progressive fatigue as the day wears on. This is a particular problem for those who ride daily, where the failure to replenish muscle glycogen leads to progressive muscle glycogen depletion and chronic fatigue.

The Century Ride

Nutritional recommendations for this ride are the model for a nutritional program. We will assume that this ride will be done once a week at 50%–80% V_{O2max}. The goal is to have a comfort-able ride, avoiding the bonk and dehydration.

There is no magic dietary program for the training period. During this time, the cyclist needs a balanced diet that meets the energy requirements of the training program. The usual distribu-tion of Calories approximates 50% carbohydrate, 10%–15% protein, and 25%–35% fat. As training intensifies and the total caloric replacement needs increase, the need for carbohydrate Calories will increase, while the fat and protein requirements do not change. As a result, it is not unusual for a competitive cyclist to take in 75%–90% of his or her daily Calories in the form of car-bohydrates.

These Calories should be eaten in a minimum of three meals a day. If caloric requirements are sufficiently high, frequent snack-ing may be necessary to avoid unwanted weight loss. In addition, the daily program should be structured so that a significant per-centage of the Calories are taken early in the day. This anticipates and provides for the metabolic needs of the day's exercise. There is some evidence that more Calories from the evening meal are preferentially directed to fat storage, and this possibility is minimized as well. As discussed previously, the immediate post-exercise period may provide an additional opportunity for replacing muscle glycogen, and snacking during those few hours is encouraged.

Although we have seen that fat can be of importance for endurance activities, the body's normal stores are more than adequate for these needs. Only training can increase free fatty acid utilization. Increasing dietary fat has no beneficial effect to force this metabolic change. In fact, there has been suggestive evidence that a high-fat diet actually decreases endurance capacity.

Proteins, although essential at a level of 40-70 grams per day, are likewise potentially harmful to a training program at higher intakes. There is is no evidence that increasing protein intake above these requirements improves muscle development, and any extra protein Calories are merely metabolized into glycogen or body fat. In addition, the by-product of this metabolism, urea, requires water for its excretion by the kidneys. This not only may have a long-term negative effect on kidney function, but also exacerbates any tendency toward dehydration.

In contrast to fats and proteins, the appropriate use of carbohydrates can enhance cycling performance and is important in a training program. A high-carbohydrate diet increases the amount of glycogen stored in the muscles and liver. This not only increases the duration of performance before exhaustion during the competitive event, but also has a positive effect during the training program itself.

A diet deficient in carbohydrates results in a gradual decline in muscle glycogen (stores are not completely rebuilt after each training session) and can produce a chronic state of fatigue. In addition, failure to replenish muscle glycogen has been associated with the development of post-exercise muscle stiffness. Both can prevent an optimal progressive training regimen. To avoid these problems, it is important that the total caloric expenditures be replaced each day and that a conscious effort be made to assure that at least 600 grams, or 2,400 Calories (based on potential muscle and liver glycogen stores) be in the form of carbohydrates. At this time there is no evidence that complex carbohydrates are superior to simple sugars for the glycogen repletion process.

As the total body energy stores, particularly muscle and liver glycogen, are so important to the overall success of a training program, there needs to be a close and conscious monitoring of the balance between energy expenditure and daily caloric intake. Daily weighing provides a check on this process and the body weight should be monitored each morning before any exercise that may cause a change in the state of hydration. Any progressive weight loss should lead to a reevaluation of the overall Calorie-replacement program.

In preparation for the event, glycogen loading can be considered. At the extreme, this is a program of 6 days duration which begins with depletion of muscle glycogen by prolonged exertion, i.e., 2–4 hours of cycling. For the next 3 days, a low-carbohydrate diet (100 grams of carbohydrate per day) is ingested. The last 3 days require a high-carbohydrate diet, consisting of 60%–70% carbohydrates, with at least 600 grams of carbohydrate per day. This replenishes the muscle glycogen stores and allows the supercompensation, or loading, to occur. Some athletes feel that the weight gain and muscle stiffness that occur with this program interferes with their performance and prefer to omit the initial exercise/depletion phase. In that case, the high-carbohydrate diet is similar to the regimen recommended for the entire training period as described above.

A balanced diet will meet all vitamin and mineral requirements during the training period. If there is any concern about becoming deficient because of unusual dietary habits or a weight-loss program, a daily multivitamin is generally considered safe. Salt replacement is usually unnecessary unless there will be an estimated fluid loss in excess of 4% BW (body weight).

If the cyclist has been on a good dietary regimen during the training period—daily replacement of Calories expended with an emphasis on carbohydrates, good hydration, and minimal exercise for the 2 days before—there are no special requirements in the immediate pre-event period (the 4 hours before competition). The pre-event meal should be eaten at least 3–4 hours before the competition begins. Like other meals of a good training diet, this meal should be high in carbohydrate (60%-70% of Calories), low in fat, and should be taken with adequate fluids. It appears that maximum benefit is gained from a 300-gram carbohydrate meal. A low residue (fiber) content and a low salt content are also recommended. If liquid food is planned, it can be taken up to 2 hours prior to the event because of more rapid stomach emptying, digestion, and absorption. This approach is preferred by some cyclists who also feel it decreases nausea.

There is evidence that a carbohydrate snack immediately prior to competition (5–10 minutes before) is helpful in prolonging the duration of exercise to exhaustion. This is only important in events lasting more than 2 hours and presumably works by protecting muscle glycogen stores in the same manner as supplements taken while exercising. It is important to time the consumption of this snack closely, as too long an interval before the event can allow digestion, absorption, and an insulin response with resulting hypoglycemia just as the event is beginning. It is for the same reason that a meal should be avoided in the critical period 4 hours before the event.

Carbohydrate supplements are important during events of more than 2 hours duration. There is no consensus on the best carbohydrate formula, but it appears that liquids with up to a 10% glucose concentration are preferable. Drinks containing complex carbohydrates may give an additional edge by supplying even more carbohydrate Calories.

It is important that carbohydrate supplements be started at the same time as the event. Once fatigue has occurred, oral glucose is much less effective in prolonging performance. There may be some latitude as to the maximum carbohydrate supplementation per hour the body can utilize. Although one study suggested that the maximum was 1 gram of glucose per minute, or 60 grams per hour (4 Calories per minute or 240 Calories per hour), recent work suggests that up to 800 grams per hour of a 20%–25% concentration may be used.[35]

Another approach to enhancing the use of both glucose stores and oral supplements is to modify the exercise intensity or the percentage of V_{O2max} at which one is performing. The relationship between glucose and FFA as an energy source for exercise is not a linear one. That is, a 20% increase in V_{O2} from 50% to 70% of V_{O2max} uses less additional glucose than an increase from 70% to 90% (see Fig. 1.2). Thus an endurance athlete can utilize additional fat, covering more miles before all body glycogen is depleted, by simply slowing down slightly. This can be of particular importance if a sprint is needed at the end of the event. As glycogen is essential both for aerobic exercise approaching 100% V_{O2max} and for any anaerobic activity, a cyclist who has used all his or her glycogen is truly "out of gas."

Fluid replacement is essential and should be started on a preventive basis within 15–20 minutes of the start of the event, particularly if weather conditions are adverse—high temperatures and very high or very low humidity. A fluid deficit of up to 2% BW does not appear to have an adverse effect on performance. However, at a deficit of 3% BW there is a decrease in endurance and at 4%–7% BW a definitive deterioration in muscle strength. Above 6% BW life-threatening complications, such as heat exhaustion and heat stroke, can occur.

One study has also demonstrated that there can be a persistent deficit in isometric and isotonic performance 4 hours after rehydration has taken place, which reconfirms the need to anticipate and regularly replace fluid losses.[21] The stomach does have its limits, however, and it appears that 800 ml, or approximately 1 quart, is the most that can be handled per hour. This volume diminishes as exercise intensity increases, and nausea and distention can occur if larger volumes are pushed. [35]

During severe conditions of temperature or humidity, or with prolonged training and competitive sessions, regular pre- and post-event weighing can help to assess the adequacy of fluid replacement. For periods of less than 4 hours, any weight loss will be primarily fluid related.

Post-event nutrition is particularly important if regular training is planned the next day. A carbohydrate drink, especially a complex carbohydrate in the 4 hours post event, is optimal. Beyond that, nutritional goals are the same as during the training period.

The following plan summarizes these recommendations. In addition to the 4-day pre-event training period, the 4-hour pre-event interval, the event itself, and the post-event period, there are recommendations for the baseline training period.

Recommended Nutrition Plan

Baseline Training Period

1. Determine daily caloric replacement needs (Table 2.2)

2. Calculate body weight in kg (BW = 0.455 × weight in lbs)

3. Formulate diet per 24 hours as follows:

Protein:

1.5 × BW = grams of protein per day

Total protein Cal = gm/protein × 4 Cal/gm

Fat:

Assume 70 gm per day based on avg. American diet

Total fat Cal = 70 gm × 9 Cal/gm = 630 Cal

Carbohydrate:

Balance of the replacement needs (in gm)

(Replacement Cal – Protein Cal – Fat Cal) ÷ 4 Cal/gm

It is advantageous to replace Calories 1–2 hours after exercise

Pre-Event Interval

4 days prior to the event:

9 gm carbohydrate/kg BW/day (approx. 600 gm/day)

balance of Cal from fat and protein (no set ratio)

limit exercise to minimum to maintain flexibility

4 hours prior to the event:

300 gm carbohydrate meal minimum (low fat)

4 minutes prior to the event:

45 gm carbohydrate (candy bar, for example)

During the Event

Calories:

regular carbohydrate replacement (start immediately

60 gm carbohydrate minimum

liquid carbohydrate preferred (i.e., sports drink)

10% concentration optimal (equivalent to cola drinks)

complex carbohydrate drinks permit additional Calories.

Liquids:

800 ml/hr

drink at 15-minute intervals

standard water bottle = 590 ml

Post-Event

3–6 gm carb/kg BW over the 4 hours immediately post event, starting first ½ hour.

600 gm carb/day for 2 days to replete muscle/liver glycogen.

Training Ride or Mountain Biking

This ride may be a 5- or 6-hour undertaking, but is different from the century or casual ride in that it is usually undertaken several times a week at a much higher percentage of V_{O2max}. The goal is not only to maximize performance and minimize risks of the bonk, but to emphasize post-event nutrition supplements to be ready for the next day's training ride.

The training diet and the meal 4 hours before the event are exactly the same as for the century ride. However, the 300-gram pre-event meal and use of a liquid carbohydrate supplement during the event are essential, because a high-percentage V_{O2max} can be sustained only by using glycogen as an energy source. If body reserves are not supplemented with oral glucose, fat metabolism will be used later in the ride with a notable decrease in performance.

As this ride may very well be one of a series of training rides, an aggressive post-ride glucose-replacement program is important. Consuming 3–6 gm of carbohydrate per kg BW over the 4- hour post-event period will maximize rebuilding of the body's reserves and avoid the gradual fatigue of overtraining that accompanies diminishing muscle and liver glycogen.

Multiple-Day Tours

This series of rides is usually done at the slower century pace (50%-60% V_{O2max}) and is a challenge because of the need to rebuild glycogen reserves daily.

The backbone of a good nutritional plan is a solid training diet that results in maximizing glycogen reserves at the start of the tour and continues to aid glycogen replacement during the tour. A good training diet can be augmented with a carbohydrate drink during the interval between rides. As in training rides, use of carbohydrate drinks during the ride (and, as this is a more leisurely event, an occasional bakery stop) will also decrease the demands for post-ride glycogen replacement.

Nutrition for the Elite Cyclist

This chapter is for those who ask the maximum of their bodies in cycling sports. While dedication and training remain the most effective methods of developing natural abilities, and although nutritional conditioning will never be a substitute for a demanding physical training program, good nutrition is essential to achieve and maintain top physical performance. Given two equally talented and trained competitors, a sound nutrition program will provide the additional edge that makes one a winner.

Not all great racing is done at top speed: Sue Notorangelo, multiple winner of the Race Across America, is riding for endurance here, and her diet has to match the demands on her body.

Track Events and Criteriums

In these events, the cyclist will be working at 80%–100% V_{O2max} for 1–2 hours, and will occasionally slip into anaerobic metabolism during a sprint.

The training diet is critical in assuring that maximum glycogen stores are available at the start of the event. A major concern is the chronic glycogen depletion that occurs with regular training when the daily diet fails to replace caloric expenditures. This is the most important aspect of nutrition for those participating in these events. And contrary to "pop" nutritionists, it is carbohydrates, not fats or protein, that are the key to success.

The 4-day pre-event period presents an opportunity to maximize the body's glycogen reserves, and a goal of at least 600 grams of carbohydrate per day assures that this will be achieved.

Although the body can provide all the glucose needed for an event of an hour or less, cyclists anticipating a slightly longer criterium or race would benefit from the 300-gram carbohydrate meal 4 hours before the competition. This is particularly true because anaerobic metabolism during a sprint is very inefficient, requiring large amounts of glucose when compared to equal aerobic energy output. The former drains the body's reserves more quickly and makes oral supplements that much more important.

Glucose supplements are of little use in a pursuit or race of less than an hour. In these events it is lack of water, with dehydration, that can be a major factor in decreased performance. However, as that 1-hour threshold is approached, glucose supplements take on increasing importance.

Post-event supplements are important to replenish body glycogen in anticipation of a return to a regular training schedule, and may decrease the muscle stiffness that results from "wringing" all the glycogen out of the muscles during extreme competition. They are of strategic importance if one is to ride in another event on the same or the following day.

Triathlons

The triathlon is any athletic contest involving three separate events done sequentially. The first triathlon was held in San Diego in 1974. Although usually considered to be a combination of swimming, cycling, and running, other sports can be substituted. To be successful competitively, a rigorous training program is essential. Because of the unique physiologic requirements, adequate nutrition is a key component of any winning strategy. [203]

As with any aerobic athletic event, improvement with training is easily documented. Unfortunately, cross training does not occur to any appreciable extent. Although there is some improvement in cardiac performance that carries over from sport to sport, the majority of the training benefit is muscle specific, i.e., related only to the muscle group being exercised.

As noted previously, training increases the muscle's capacity for carbohydrate and fatty acid metabolism so that the percentage of energy from fat metabolism is increased and the production of lactate decreased at any submaximal workload. This results in a slower rate of glycogen depletion and increased endurance.

As a result of the intense training for three separate events, daily caloric expenditures are high, and the time available for eating or replacement minimized. This places an extra burden on the triathlete to avoid chronic glycogen depletion and training fatigue. A high-carbohydrate training diet that matches Calories eaten to those expended is a key to maximizing training effectiveness.

There are two aspects of nutrition unique to a triathlete's training program. The first is the strategy of eating and drinking during training sessions for the specific purpose of developing a tolerance for refueling during the actual competition events. The second is the use of the 4-hour post-exercise period for rapid muscle glycogen replacement to maximize recovery, particularly when there are several discrete training sessions per day.

During the long periods of training, the triathlete can easily lose 2 liters of fluid per hour. As thirst often lags behind the actual state of hydration, it is easy to develop a state of mild, chronic dehydration. This puts the athlete at increased risk of decreased performance the day of the event. This risk can be minimized by periodically checking body weights and urine specific gravity (concentration) during the training program.

The nutrition recommendations for the 4 days and 4 hours before the competition parallel those for a century rider (see Chapter 4).

During competition, the benefits of carbohydrate supplementation parallel those of any endurance activity, but there are unique requirements for the triathlete as well. If the entire event will last less than 2 hours, minimal carbohydrate supplementation will be needed, although fluid replacement is essential. In a longer event, carbohydrates are a necessity, but need to be compatible with the event. Thus during the swimming portion, no eating, either liquid or solid, is possible. During cycling, solid foods can be eaten early on with a transition to liquid carbohydrate supplements an hour before the start of the run, while liquids are optimal during the run itself.

Because of the duration of some triathlons, electrolyte replacement may be prudent. Hyponatremia (a low blood sodium level) does not appear to be a problem in triathlons of less than 4 hours; it is an occasional problem in those 4–8 hours long and a definite risk in triathlons lasting more than 8 hours. Using an average loss of 2 liters of sweat per hour, and figuring a conservative salt content one quarter that of body fluid, a goal of 1–2 grams of salt per hour as replacement has been suggested.

There are no unique requirements for post-competition carbohydrate or electrolyte repletion beyond those of the century rider covered in Chapter 4.

Finally, several studies of micronutrient needs have suggested that triathletes may, as a group, have marginal total body zinc levels, and as many as 50% may have latent iron deficiency. No other specific vitamin or mineral deficiencies have been noted. These minerals can have gastrointestinal and other toxic side effects in high doses, and supplements should be taken only after discussion with a knowledgeable authority.

Multiday Stage Races

The ultimate example of a multiday staged road race is the Tour de France. This race is typically 3 weeks long, covering roughly 4,000 kilometers. The average energy intake of the participants is 5,700 Calories per day with almost 50% of the Calories taken while on the bike. Overall, 70% of Calories are from carbohydrates, and 30% of the carbohydrate Calories are from carbohydrate-rich liquids.[211]

Studies of actual Tour participants were used to develop a laboratory model of similar exercise intensity over a 6-day period. [212] In this a model, 1,500 cc of a carbohydrate-rich solution (20% weight volume long-chain glucose polymer) was used to supplement the high-carbohydrate diet. Several interesting findings were:

☐ When prolonged intensive cycling increased energy expenditures above 4,600 Calories per day, the athletes were unable to consume enough conventional food to replace caloric expenditures.

☐ Using a concentrated carbohydrate solution did permit energy balance to be maintained.

☐ Protein requirements under exercise circumstances were in excess of 1.5 gmper kg of body weight per day.

☐ The use of a carbohydrate-rich diet and concentrated carbohydrate solution to maintain energy balance decreased protein oxidation to a level requiring a protein intake of 1.5–1.8 gm protein per kg of body weight per day.

In an elegant follow-up study using a similar physiologic model and carbohydrate supplement , they demonstrated:

☐ The use of a 20% complex carbohydrate drink spared intramuscular glycogen and increased exercise time to exhaustion.

☐ Post-exercise use of the carbohydrate supplement permitted glycogen replacement to reach supercompensation levels within 24 hours.

☐ Trained individuals had an increased lactate clearance and also an increased capacity to metabolize intramuscular fat.

Based on these findings, which confirm the physiologic studies presented in the first two chapters, the following recommendations can be made:

☐ The training diet remains important and may require a carbohydrate-rich supplement (20% weight/volume, 1,500 cc per day) to maintain energy balance, depending on the level of training. This is particularly true of the 4 days prior to the start of the event.

☐ A 300-gram solid carbohydrate meal should be eaten 4 hours before the race.

☐ A concentrated carbohydrate drink (10%–20% weight to volume) should be started at the beginning of the race and continued at a rate of up to a liter per hour during the race.

☐ The post-race period is critical to muscle glycogen repletion in preparation for the next day. At least a liter of 20% weight to volume carbohydrate solution should be taken in the first 2–4 hours post ride.

Analysis of micronutrient and vitamin levels in the competitors were little different from those in triathletes, and recommendations for vitamin and mineral supplementation are the same in both groups.

CHAPTER 6

Carrying Your Calories

Now that you've made a decision on your fuel for the day, it's time to review the alternatives available for carrying it on your bike trip. There are several options—each with its own advantages and disadvantages, as summarized in Table 6.1. Although there are some minor disadvantages associated with carrying food on the bike, a little planning can eliminate the rough edges.

Packaging and Packing

With commercial products this is rarely a problem, since durable packaging appears to be part of successful food marketing. However, repacking foods purchased in bulk or packaging those

Racktop packs are suitable for carrying food, since it does not get pushed, banged and damaged in this location.

personally prepared at home can be a challenge, especially with liquid or semisolid items.

In competitive events, where even a small distraction can cost valuable seconds, packaging is a major consideration in planning for caloric replacement. For the recreational rider who intends to eat while on the bike, safety is the issue, since even a momentary lapse in concentration can lead to a fall. For those planning a relaxed outing with a stop to eat, packaging is important to prevent leaks during transportation and to maintain the appetizing appearance of the food.

There is no universal answer to the packaging challenge, as each food and type of event has its own unique requirements. In competitive events, where time is of the essence, less is truly more, and foods such as cookies and dried fruits that need no wrappers are favored. If the event allows a few additional seconds for eating, but still requires eating on the bike, loosely wrapped nonliquid items can be added to the menu. But beware of those prepackaged items that come in indestructible plastic and require two hands and scissors to open. For the picnic crowd, self-sealing Tupperware-type containers are best, and come in various sizes and shapes.

Once individual items have been packaged, they need to be packed for the event. For the single rider with a one-course meal this is rarely a problem, but for larger groups and multi-course meals some planning is necessary. The effect of vibration and shifting or migration of containers needs to be anticipated. This can be controlled by using picnic accessories such as napkins or a table-cloth for packing material, or with alternatives such as loosely "balled" newspaper and foam rubber. The latter can be precut to protect not only food containers but also glassware for those planning the truly elegant outing.

Packaging Snacks

Packaging of small food items is an often-neglected but very important part of a successful cycling nutrition program. Such aspects as transportability, accessibility, and portion size need to be considered. The snacks to be consumed while riding should be in a form that is durable and will transport well until eaten. Prepare or purchase them in bite-size pieces, and package them for easy access when needed. Snacks readily adapted to this program include hard cookies, fig bars, apple slices, orange slices, and some hard bars such as granola bars.

Plastic sandwich bags make a simple packaging for snack foods that are durable but might crumble or melt in your pocket. They do not work well for multiple servings, as it is difficult to open the bag and separate the contents while continuing to concentrate on the road. For this reason, single-portion packaging is recommended for competitive riding or whenever fast feeding on the bike is planned. The ideal model is the trusty banana, which must have been developed by a cyclist. It resists the destructive forces often applied to items carried in a jersey pocket, is packaged in a biodegradable wrapper, is readily accessible using one hand and the teeth, and adapts easily to single-bite portions.

Carrying Solid Food

The jersey pocket allows the simplest, safest, and most ready access to food while riding, and it remains the preference of competitive riders. It has the advantage of easy accessibility with minimal

Two extremes for carrying food: in the jersey pocket, left, and in pannier bags, right, for short and long trips, respectively.

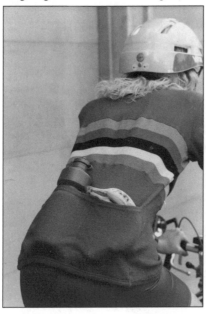 

effects on bike handling and aerodynamics. The disadvantage lies in the limited carrying capacity. The alternative in competitive events is the musette, or food bag, handed to the riders at predetermined locations. This is suited to long-distance events where the bulk and weight of the food needed to replace the Calories expended would not fit in the pockets of a cycling jersey, or might have a negative impact on performance if it were.

The fanny pack is gaining increased acceptance by competitive long distance and recreational bikers. It has been used by cross-country skiers for years and, because it is attached by a waist belt, has the advantage of leaving the shoulders and upper body free. The weight is carried quite low and thus has no effect on shoulder fatigue. This pack can hold more than the pockets of a jersey, yet it can be accessed while riding if needed. Although the pack is usually worn in back to eliminate any interference when assuming the aerodynamic drop position while cycling, it can be pulled around to the front with minimal effort while sitting in the upright position. Then either one or both hands can be used to open the zipper and remove the food. A disadvantage is that the pack is at the same level as the jersey pockets, which essentially eliminates their use for food storage. The cumbersome maneuver described above needs to be repeated each time food is removed, and in the long run it is less efficient than using a bike pack and transferring to the jersey pockets during occasional brief stops.

The handlebar bag has the advantage of being readily accessible, and, with some caution, it can be opened while moving. It does increase wind drag and affects steering responsiveness when loaded.

There are various other bike packs available for carrying food, but all suffer from the disadvantage of being inaccessible while riding. These can carry larger quantities, and, being attached to the bike, they don't hinder the rider in any riding positions or increase body fatigue. Their disadvantages include an increase in the frontal surface area and wind drag, and a decrease in the responsiveness and maneuverability of the bike. The traditional backpack is another possibility, but is uncomfortable on longer rides. The shoulders are a weak area for many riders, and the stress of a loaded backpack can accentuate this. For this reason it is recommended only for short trips when no alternatives are available.

Bike packs, in order of increasing capacity, include the seat bag, rack-top pack, front panniers and rear panniers. The seat bag, or saddle bag, though not as popular in the United States as it is in Britain, is available in a wide variety of sizes. It can be quite small (holding no more than a spare inner tube and a candy bar) or large enough for a full meal. The saddle bag's position is relatively aerodynamic and has a minimal effect on bike handling and performance.

The rack-top pack carries more than does a handlebar bag and most seat bags, is slightly more aerodynamic in its location behind the rider and seat post, and has less effect on handling characteristics. It is my favorite to carry food for group outings. The rack-top pack requires a bike rack (as do panniers).

Panniers have as their advantage the quantity of food and other items that can be carried. They have a significant wind-drag effect, and when loaded are heavy enough to influence bike handling significantly. They are available in small versions intended to be used on the front, and as larger models intended to be used with a luggage rack in the rear, though the smaller version also fits in the back.

The ultimate pack, mentioned for completeness, is the sagwagon—a car or van following the cyclists. This method of transportation allows almost unlimited carrying capacity, including the bike and rider if all is not going well. It represents the ultimate in rider comfort, as no additional weight needs to be carried on the bike or by the rider. It presents no access problems, provides the ability to obtain food while moving (in the form of a quick hand-off), and can actually cut down on wind drag if drafting maneuvers are considered. Its major disadvantage is a philosophical one for those cyclists who wish to be truly self-propelled. For off-road cycling, the sagwagon is of course only of very limited use, as it cannot follow the riders or meet up with them except in those places where they return to civilization.

Table 6.1 Comparison of carrying gear

Item	carrying capacity	rider comfort	access	air drag	bike handling
Jersey pocket	+	–	++++	ME	ME
Backpack	+++	– – –	0	ME	–
Fanny pack	++	–	++	ME	ME
Seat pack	+	ME	0	–	ME
Handlebar bag	++	ME	+	– – –	– –
Rack pack	+++	ME	0	– –	–
Panniers	++++	ME	0	– – –	– – –

Legend to Table 6.1

ME= minimal effect   + = relatively better

0 = no effect   – = relatively worse

Carrying Fluids

Unlike solid foods, there are limited options for carrying fluids. All require a closed plastic bottle which is generally carried on the bike in a cage or rack. The cage is usually attached to either the down tube or the seat tube, but can also be attached to the handlebar stem for easier access. On occasion, the water bottle can be carried in a jersey pocket, usually when an additional or reserve bottle is to be used. It should be carried in the middle pocket of the traditional three-pocket jersey to minimize the tendency to slide around to either side.

The traditional water bottle spigot is a nipple with a slide closure which drains directly from the top of the bottle. This requires the bottle and head be tipped while drinking— with the attendant risk of getting a mouthful of air and water when the bottle is partially empty and not tipped quite far enough. A greater danger lies in the need to take your eyes off the road while drinking this way. A major advance is the use of a drain tube extending to the bottom of the bottle, eliminating the need to tip the bottle to drink. It also eliminates the air surge until the bottle is completely empty. An additional refinement is the use of a hand bulb pump and extension tubing to allow the bottle to remain in the cage while manual air pressurization delivers fluid directly into the mouth.

CHAPTER 7

Where to Eat

Now that we have decided what to eat and how to carry it, it's time to consider the topic of where to eat. Evolution has adapted humans to eat in all positions and under almost all conditions. Since this book was written to increase the enjoyment of cycling, let's look at a few tips to liven up your tour or event.

Eating on the Bike

The most common place to eat while cycling is—you guessed it— on the bike. This goes for the recreational cyclist as well as the competitive rider. The major consideration is safety; eating while on the bike takes some practice and concentration. During practice rides, be sure to note both the effects of a mouthful of food on breathing as well as the ease with which food can be aspirated into the windpipe. The following should also be kept in mind while eating to avoid unnecessary risks:

If you tour with sagwaggon support, eating is easy, providing you don't miss the food stop.

1. Slow down.

2. Increase concentration on the road, anticipating upcoming obstacles or hazards.

3. In a pace line, eat when at the end, not in the middle or while pulling.

4. On hilly terrain, eat after you crest the hill, not while climbing.

If these simple measures are considered, it won't be necessary to stop to eat.

Roadside Shops

Bakeries are the second most common eating spots. Seasoned tourers will often use a bakery as an intermediate goal to break up the tedium of a long ride. It is wise to space these bakery stops at 2-hour intervals, when muscle glycogen stores are usually approaching exhaustion and need replenishing. A good tour or ride leader will often scout out the best bakeries and plan the day accordingly. These stops minimize the need to carry extra weight and bulk on the bike. In fact, it is the availability of bakeries and the associated opportunity to "carbo replete" en route that provide the major incentives for many Saturday riders.

The use of bed-and-breakfast, or B&B, accommodations is an extension of the bakery concept for the multiple-day tour. These stops provide comfortable lodgings and a pleasant breakfast before heading off for the first bakery. They minimize the need to carry camping gear and can provide a goal for the tour if they are in a unique setting. As with bakeries, the wise tour leader will often plan the trip around the most desirable B&Bs, knowing that the psychological diversion of the evening will often make the next day's riding that much more pleasant.

Sagwagon

When a sagwagon is used, and particularly when the driver is someone who wants to participate in the group camaraderie but either can't or does not want to ride, a modification of the B&B approach is very successful. In this situation, the cyclists set off after deciding on a predetermined meeting point for the midday meal break. The sagwagon driver then has the option of sleeping in, lounging around, or reconnoitering the local gift shops before setting out in the morning.

The sagwagon carries the food and whatever else is needed to provide the opportunity for a major midday meal, ranging from a simple picnic to a regal affair with all the trimmings, including real plates, flatware, and glasses. After a relaxed lunch, the driver proceeds to the night's lodging and again has extra time to relax before the bike group arrives. This approach opens up many options for cycling families, particularly when there are divergent goals and abilities. The fact that a motor vehicle is available also extends the possibilities for the evening meal.

Picnic Spots

The ultimate challenge is often picking an appropriate spot for your picnic, whether supported by a sagwagon or when carrying the food entirely on the bike. Fortunately, there are limitless possibilities. While bakeries are in predetermined locations, a picnic can be set almost anywhere. A quiet spot off the highway is preferable, and additional rustic trappings such as a stream or a lake can add to the atmosphere.

An important aspect of nutrition: finding the perfect picnic site.

Most people have their own mental image of the ideal setting for a picnic, and with the miles of country roads and off-road terrain now accessible by mountain bike, you will find many superb spots along your way or just a little off the beaten track. It is the multitude of possibilities that makes bike touring and the picnics that go along with it so appealing to the adventuresome.

CHAPTER 8

Practical Tips

In previous chapters we used an understanding of physiology and nutrition to develop a nutrition program for cyclists. Then we reviewed the issues of packaging and transporting food on the bike. In this chapter we'll review "road-tested" practical tips from cyclists to help you customize your cycling nutrition plan.

Snacks and Light Meals

Foods in this category form the backbone of any serious cycling program, providing variety and an occasional psychological lift for those out on a pleasure ride. The difference between a snack and a light meal is often difficult to define, but hinges on the factors of quantity and quality, i.e.:

1. How much is eaten at any one time?

2. Do you want to eat on the bike or stop to do so?

The philosophy toward food breaks varies with one's goals. Recreational riders with the luxury of time will stop to enjoy their snacks, while those in the competitive mode will begin a program of snacking on the bike early in the ride in anticipation of the delay in stomach emptying that occurs with strenuous exercise. Any Calories absorbed will delay glycogen depletion with the subsequent onset of fatigue, or the "bonk."

The secret for maximum performance in events that last more than 2 hours (the time at which muscle glycogen depletion occurs) is to snack frequently, at least every 20–30 minutes. A successful program requires a compromise between eating enough to prevent hunger and avoiding the pitfall of "if a little is good, a lot must be better," with its accompanying risk of stomach distention, bloating and nausea, and deterioration in performance.

To apply this concept to your program, refer to Table 2.3 (Chapter 2) and, based on your own goals and abilities, make a rough estimate of your caloric requirements per hour. Next, decide on an eating schedule—every 15 or 20 minutes is a practical compromise. Then, using the suggestions below, a specific program can be tailored to meet your caloric needs. The final step is a road test. This is essential, since physiologic and digestive functions vary from person to person and may require individual refinements to meet your specific needs or preferences.

Foods in this section can also be used in the pre-race meal. If so, they should be eaten at least 4 hours prior to the start of the event. This assures that your stomach will be empty and that the bulk of digestion and absorption will have occurred before the stress of vigorous activity causes the inevitable slow-down in these processes.

Snack Survey

In the belief that there are common foods preferred by most riders, both competitive and recreational, a survey of snack foods was undertaken, including a review of several cycling magazines, to establish what these might be. The diversity of responses was a surprise—it appears that everyone has his or her own favorite. However, there was a pattern in the groups of food. Dried fruits were the most common—presumably because of their high caloric content, the ease with which bite-size portions could be prepared, and their relatively indestructible nature when carried on a long ride. Table 8.1 summarizes the results of this survey and include the Calories per average serving. For perspective, remember that at 15 miles per hour a 165-lb rider expends 400 Calories per hour.

Two prepared "delicacies" hold promise, but the exact caloric content could not be determined due to individual variation in preparation. The first was a sandwich of jelly and cream cheese. The second, a mixture of peaches, honey, and water in a plastic bag, emphasizes that there is plenty of room for experimentation in the snack area.

Another option is the commercial "powerbars." Although they are advertised as providing a particularly potent combination of ingredients, they are no more effective on a gram-for-gram basis as an energy booster than other carbohydrate snacks. Advantages are that they are prepackaged and readily available commercially as well as offering another taste and texture option for a snack.

There are some foods to avoid (or at least leave to the end of your experimental list). The stress of vigorous exercise has a stimulating effect on the digestive tract, and the more vigorous the exercise (or more out of shape the rider) the greater this effect. Certain foods can accentuate this normal physiologic reflex including dairy products and spicy, greasy, or oily foods. Moderation is the key to success in snack planning. The best advice is to start off with small amounts of those foods that sound appealing, and use your own individual response to decide on their place in your nutrition program. Additional suggestions for snack foods can be found in Chapter 10.

Beverages

It is safe to say that the single biggest mistake of many competitive athletes is the failure to replace the fluid losses associated with exercise. This is aggravated in cycling, because moving air promotes rapid skin evaporation and decreases the sense of perspiring, leading to a false impression of minimal fluid loss. For a successful ride, it is essential that fluid replacement be started early and continued on a regular basis.

During vigorous exercise, the sensation of thirst lags well behind fluid replacement needs. As a result, once you notice that you are thirsty there will already be a significant fluid deficit to overcome. On a hot day, a minimum of 4–5 ounces of fluid should be taken every 15 minutes from the start of exercise. A practical way to determine if you are taking adequate fluid replacement is to weigh yourself before and after a long ride. A drop of a pound or two won't impair performance, but greater weight loss indicates the need to change your replacement routine. As you customize a program to your personal needs, remember that a pint of liquid weighs roughly one pound.

Several factors influence fluid replacement requirements. An obvious one is the day's temperature. Another is the fluid content of your snacks. If fresh fruits with a high liquid content, such as oranges, apples, grapes, or peaches, are being eaten, fluid intake can be scaled back accordingly. Alcoholic beverages should be strictly avoided. Alcohol is not only a mild diuretic, accentuating the tendency to dehydrate, but also interferes with performance through its negative effect on glucose metabolism in the liver.

Any sugar in the replacement fluids is usually considered a bonus for the cyclist. Because liquids are readily emptied from the stomach, this sugar is quickly absorbed into the bloodstream and transported to the muscles, where it is available as an alternative

Table 8.1 Preferred Bicycle Snacks

Food	Quantity	Calories	Carbs
Cookies (generic)	2 small or 1 large	105	15
Fig Newton	1	50	20
Chips Ahoy	1	65	9
Oreo	1	47	7
Graham cracker	1	30	5
Animal cracker	1	11	2
Ginger snap	1	30	6
Vanilla wafer	1	19	3
Fresh fruit			
banana	4 oz (1 avg. size)	100	26
pear	4 oz	98	25
grapes	1 cup	57	16
orange	4 oz (1 avg. size)	65	16
apple	4 oz (1 avg. size)	80	21
peach	4 oz (1 avg. size)	37	10
cantaloupe	1 cup, pieces	57	13
Dried fruit			
raisins	1/3 cup	150	40
apricots	10 halves	83	22
prunes	5 whole	100	53
apples	1/4 cup, pieces	52	13
figs	5 whole	238	61
fruit roll-up	1/2 oz (1 avg. size)	50	12
Candy bar (generic)	1 oz	130	16
Gum drop	1 oz	98	25
Baked potato	1 avg. size	220	51
Pastries			
doughnut	1 avg. size	125	14
eclair	1 avg. size	239	23
muffin	1 avg. size	126	20
toast	1 slice	64	11
plain bagel	1	163	31
Rice pudding	1/2 cup	193	35
Rice (cooked)	1 cup	223	50
Yogurt	1 cup	140	15

to muscle glycogen stores. Following the same reasoning, drinks containing glucose polymers are even more advantageous, since they permit a higher caloric "density"—the number of Calories per ounce of fluid.

There have been no studies confirming benefits of fruit drinks (which contain the sugar fructose) over glucose drinks. Although fructose sugars need less insulin to enter the muscle cell, this appears to be of minimal or no practical benefit to cycling performance. Taste alone appears to be the advantage of fruit drinks.

Until recently, it was thought that a 2.5% concentration of glucose or glucose polymer molecules was the maximum tolerated by the digestive tract without delaying stomach emptying and causing nausea. A recent study on cyclists has shown normal stomach emptying with 6%–8% solutions, but when the concentrations were pushed above 11%, the expected nausea occurred.

In summary, drinking plain water at a rate of 1 quart per hour is adequate for rides of 1½–2 hours. On longer rides, where the body's glycogen stores will be approaching exhaustion, glucose supplements assume increased importance. An 8%–10% sugar concentration appears to be the maximum tolerated. Glucose polymers offer the advantage of increasing the number of Calories per quart without an unpalatable sweet taste. Table 8.2 compares the commercial drinks currently available. It is interesting to note that the old standbys, such as apple juice and cola

Many cyclists' favorite snack. There are other ways of getting the same Calories, but none as widely advertised as this one.

drinks, have that magic maximum concentration of 10% and are very cost effective per Calorie provided.

The physiological benefits, if any, of glucose polymers over simple sugars in replacement drinks are still being clarified. Although there is little question that more Calories can be ingested per quart of fluid, there has not been a clear performance advantage when evaluated under controlled conditions.[51] At this time, the major benefit of the polymers appears to be the absence of the sweet taste and nauseating properties of high-concentration glucose drinks, eliminating this barrier to maintaining a high fluid intake.

Picnic and Gourmet Food

Foods in this category—recipes for a few are in Chapter 10—will be of interest to recreational cyclists, particularly those who "bike to eat." This group appreciates the rewards that go with maintaining fitness and replacing the Calories burned with aerobic exercise. Some of these foods can also be adapted for endurance activity, particularly if taste fatigue develops from the "same old foods" on those long century rides. Be warned, however, that the higher fat content in some recipes makes them not only heavy to carry on the bike for a long trip, but may also create the same sensation in the stomach.

The picnic ride is a gala social occasion compared to training sessions and competitive cycling. This is the event that appeals to the whole family and those friends who only occasionally ride a bike. To the non-cyclist, the picnic becomes the main focus, while the cycling itself remains an excuse for the outing. An additional benefit of the modest exercise associated with the ride, as opposed to vigorous exercise, is that it stimulates the appetite and enhances the taste of the meal that follows.

Packaging may be a major problem for the picnic cyclist. It is often easier to bring the raw materials and create the finished product on site, rather than to attempt transporting the completed dish. The best results are obtained if one keeps an open and innovative mind and uses self-sealing containers that approximate the size and shape of the food being prepared. If all else fails, remember that every meal on a picnic or camping trip tastes like gourmet fare, even if it's a little lopsided.

Table 8.2 Comparison of sports drinks (courtesy BICYCLING)

Sports Drink	Main Ingredients	Recommended Concentration	Sodium*	Other Electrolytes*	Calories*	Cost ($)*
BODY FUEL 100	Glucose Polymers	0.3%	63 mg	None	13	.81
BODY FUEL 450	Glucose Polymers, Fructose	4%	200 mg	Potassium - 50 mg	100	.57
CARBO PLUS	Glucose Polymers	16%	13 mg	Potassium - 250 mg, Magnesium - 250 mg	425	1.83
EXCEED — FLUID REPLACEMENT AND ENERGY DRINK	Glucose Polymers (Polycose brand), Fructose	7.2%	165 mg	Potassium - 140 mg, Magnesium - 15 mg	170	.73
FILA FITNESS	Fructose, Sucrose	6.9%	138 mg	Potassium - 38 mg, Chloride - 244 mg	139	1.25
GATORADE	Sucrose, Glucose	6%	275 mg	Potassium - 63 mg	125	.99
GOOKINAID E.R.G.	Glucose	5.7%	175 mg	Potassium - 250 mg	113	.47
MAX	Glucose Polymers	7.5%	38 mg	None	175	.47
PRIPPS PLUSS	Sucrose	7.4%	163 mg	Potassium - N/A	175	.47
RECHARGE	Fructose (From fruit juices)	7.6%	75 mg	Potassium - 213 mg	180	.99
RPM ENERGY DRINK	Fructose	7.6%	0 mg	Potassium - 175 mg	175	.62
TOUR DE FRANCE CARBOPLEX II	Glucose Polymers, Fructose	5.9%	6 mg	None	113	.45
TOUR DE FRANCE REHYDRATE	Fructose	4.4%	250 mg	Potassium - 175 mg	100	.47
ULTRA-ENERGY	Glucose Polymers, Sucrose, Lactose, Dextrose	23%	N/A	Magnesium - N/A, Calcium - N/A, Potassium - N/A	500	5.00
VITALADE	Fructose	10%	0 mg	Potassium - 233 mg	215	.78
CARBONATED COLA	High-fructose corn syrup; Sucrose	10.4%	25 mg	Potassium - 6.2 mg, Magnesium - 6.2 mg	260	.83
APPLE JUICE	Fructose, Glucose	11.7%	20 mg	Potassium - 740 mg, Magnesium - 20 mg	300	.95

*Per standard 20-oz. water bottle filled to top.

Bacterial growth and food poisoning can be a problem with some foods if they are not prepared and handled properly. This applies especially to dairy products, poultry, eggs, fish, mayonnaise, and cream-filled pastries. The associated risk is minimized by following several simple steps. First, by preparing the food properly, using clean utensils and fresh ingredients, the chances of bacterial contamination are reduced. The second line of defense is complete cooking, which kills any bacteria that may be present. Finally, keeping the food cool after preparation slows down the growth of any bacteria that have escaped the initial two steps. It is essential to keep your prepared foods refrigerated until the last possible minute and to use insulated styrofoam containers for transportation to help keep them cool. Even with these precautions, it is best to eat prepared foods within four to six hours of preparation or refrigeration.

Picnic Types

There are three different philosophies for the cycling picnic—the spontaneous picnic, the brown bag picnic, and the elegant picnic. The spontaneous or minimalist approach emphasizes off-the-shelf foods, and such a meal can be put together in any supermarket or grocery store. It includes ready-to-eat items such as cheese, nuts, crackers, bread, canned paté, marinated mushrooms or artichokes, fruits, vegetables, and dips.

The brown bag picnic is centered around a sandwich of fresh bread and sliced meats assembled at the picnic site. For an extra touch, a salad can be easily prepared, with the dressing added later to help keep it fresh. While this picnic can be planned walking the aisles of the supermarket, it is of immeasurable help to have access to a good delicatessen.

Finally, there is the elegant, or gourmet, picnic. This is the epitome of cycling picnics and requires prior planning and preparation time in the kitchen. Of course, any ingredients mentioned above for the spontaneous picnic can be included in this meal as well.

To aid in preparing the menu, whether minimalist or gourmet, the picnic is divided into four courses. These include:

1. appetizer or soup

2. main course

3. dessert

4. beverage

If you have an item in mind for each course, you're on your way to a successful outing.

After the food is prepared or purchased and the group is ready to set off for the memorable event, be sure to consult a final checklist. This is essential for successful picnic planning and has saved many an outing (and friendship). The following covers the necessities:

1. ground sheet or tablecloth

2. utensils, plates, and glasses or cups

3. bottle opener (or corkscrew)

4. thermos (or ice) for cold drinks

5. sharp knife

6. light cutting board or serving platter

7. napkins, paper towels (or washcloth in ziploc bag)

8. candles, matches

9. trash bag

10. insect repellent, suntan cream (or, where the climate dictates it, rain shelter)

Now that you have all the ingredients together, you're on your way to a pleasant aspect of biking that's often overlooked—the bicycle picnic. Enjoy!

International Travel

International travel presents two unique challenges. The first is finding foods both high in carbohydrate and compatible with the cyclist's digestive tract. Although exploring the local foods and spices in foreign lands is part of the adventure of international travel, the larger quantities of interesting dishes needed to replace Calories spent during the day's ride can occasionally lead to GI distress. Fortunately, carbohydrates are the mainstay of nutrition in third world countries and are found in many forms and dishes. With that variety, a little common sense is all that is needed.

A second concern relates to the possibility of traveler's diarrhea (food poisoning, tourista, Montezuma's revenge) from a bacterial infection. Again, common sense goes a long way to minimize the risks. Eat in established restaurants rather than purchasing from street vendors; disinfect your own water or use bottled water, if there is any question of sterility.

However, as even a minor case of diarrhea can be devastating when you are depending on your own legs to get you through the day, you may wish to talk to your doctor about preventive antibiotics, particularly if you are traveling in a third world country. There are two recommended approaches. The favored is to use two Pepto Bismol tablets four times a day for prevention, and to carry a supply of an antibiotic should diarrhea occur. The other, to be considered if the risks are extremely high and the planned trip is shorter than two weeks, is to take an antibiotic such as doxycycline or trimethoprim-sulfa daily for the duration of the trip. There are pros and cons to each approach, and your physician should be able to give you further advice.

CHAPTER 9

Training Diet

The training diet has been addressed earlier in general terms. A diet deficient in carbohydrates will result in a gradual decline in muscle glycogen, a decrease in performance, and, possibly a chronic state of fatigue. It is important that total caloric expenditures be replaced each day.

Most athletes focus their energy on the physical aspects of a training program and spend little time on their meal menus. As a result, it is a challenge for them to maintain a balanced, high-carbohydrate diet during the training period. This chapter provides a practical approach to this problem.

During training it is important to eat a wide variety of foods to maximize nutrition and take advantage of the micronutrients that may be missed by eating the same foods every day. Rice, pasta, grains, and beans along with a variety of fresh fruits and vegetables form the center of the meal, while meat and desserts play a supporting role.

The following sample menu provides 2,000 Calories, with 60% from carbohydrates. It is designed to be modified using an "exchange" program and for that purpose is divided into groups of similar foods (see Tables 9.1 and 9.2). When you increase the

Table 9.1 Exchange List

groups (gm)	carb (gm)	protein (gm)	fat (gm)	Cal	No. in simple 2,000-Cal diet
Starch/Bread	15	3	trace	80	12
Meat (lean)	—	7	5	75	4
Vegetable	5	2	—	25	4
Fruit	15	—	—	60	6
Milk (skim)	12	8	trace	90	2

total number of Calories above 2,000 Calories per 24 hours, the number of servings from the high-carbohydrate groups should be increased preferentially. This will increase the relative percentage of carbohydrates in the daily diet and will keep the total fat at a healthy and relatively low level.

Table 9.2 Exchange Groups

Starch/bread

½ cup pasta or barley

⅓ cup cooked rice or cooked beans

1 small potato (or ½ cup mashed)

½ cup corn, peas, or winter squash

1 slice bread or 1 roll

½ English muffin, bagel, or hamburger/hotdog bun

½ cup cooked cereal

¾ cup dry cereal (unsweetened)

5 crackers

3 cups popcorn, unbuttered, not cooked in oil

Meat

1 oz lean, skinless poultry, fish, or meat

    1 chicken leg or thigh = 2 oz

    1 small pork chop = 3 oz

    1 small hamburger = 3 oz

    1 medium fish fillet = 3 oz.

¼ cup cottage cheese

¼ cup canned salmon or tuna

1 tbsp. peanut butter

1 egg

1 oz lowfat cheese

Vegetable

½ cup cooked vegetables

1 cup raw vegetables
½ cup tomato/vegetable juice

Fruit
1 fresh medium fruit
1 cup berries or melon
½ cup canned fruit in juice without sugar
½ cup fruit juice
¼ cup dried fruit

Milk
1 cup skim milk
1 cup plain lowfat yogurt

Sample 2,000-Calorie Diet

Breakfast
¾ cup orange juice
¾ cup cold cereal (unsweetened) with ½ cup milk
2 slices whole grain toast
1 tsp. margarine or butter and preserves
½ cup lowfat yogurt with
¾ cup sliced strawberries

Lunch

2 oz shaved turkey

2 slices whole grain bread

1 tbsp. mayonnaise

lettuce

3 slices tomato

1½ cup mixed fruit salad or

1 whole apple, banana, or orange

3 ginger snap cookies

1 cup milk

Dinner

1½ cup cooked spaghetti with 1 cup meat sauce

1 tbsp. Parmesan

1 slice Italian bread

1 tsp. margarine or olive oil

2 cups tossed salad

2 tbsp. low-calorie dressing or

a sprinkle of raspberry vinegar and grind of black pepper

Snack 1

½ cup frozen yogurt or iced milk with

¾ cup sliced peaches

Snack 2

3 cups air-popped popcorn

Snack 3

1 small orange

CHAPTER 10

Recipes

In this final chapter, you will find a collection of recipes that are particularly suitable for cycling snacks, drinks and picnics.

The recipes marked with asterisks (* —— *) are those that can be prepared easily away from home, while the others require more extensive preparation in the kitchen.

Snack Recipes

George's Bars
¼ lb margarine or butter
4 eggs, beaten
1 cup flour (optional: ½ as whole wheat flour)
½ teaspoon baking powder
1 teaspoon salt
1¾ cup sugar (optional: ½ as brown sugar)
2 cups dates (or raisins, other dried fruits)
2½ cups chopped walnuts
3 tablespoons molasses (optional)

Preheat oven to 350° F.
Melt butter and cool slightly.
Add eggs.
Sift together flour, baking powder, salt, and sugar and add to eggs/shortening mix.
Combine fruits and nuts with batter.
Spread approximately 1-inch thick in 2 greased pans.
Bake 30 minutes.
Cool, cut into bars.

Crispie Treats
¼ cup margarine or butter
10 oz package (about 40) regular marshmallows
6 cups toasted rice cereal
1 cup raisins or dried fruit (optional)
½ cup peanuts or other nuts (optional)

Melt butter or margarine in large saucepan over low heat.
Add marshmallows and stir until completely melted.
Remove from heat.
Add cereal. Stir until well coated.
Using buttered spatula, press mixture into 13 x 9 x 2-inch pan.
Cut when cool.

Power Balls
1 cup graham cracker crumbs
1 cup toasted rice cereal
½ cup uncooked oatmeal (optional)
raisins, carob chips, nuts (optional)
peanut butter (room temperature)

Mix all ingredients except peanut butter in food processor.
Add peanut butter until a it forms a ball.
Hand form to desired size and shape.

Muffins

Muffins may come closest to the ideal cycling snack. They are
high in carbohydrate and allow the flexibility to add, subtract, or
substitute ingredients to meet individual tastes. In addition, they
are easy to carry and are an ideal single portion size.

Oatmeal Raisin Muffins
1½ cups flour (whole wheat if desired)
1 cup uncooked oatmeal
1 tablespoon baking powder
3 tablespoons sugar (or 2 tablespoons honey)
½ cup raisins (or other dried fruit)
¼ cup walnuts (optional)
1 egg (or 2 egg whites)

1 cup milk
¼ cup vegetable oil (or ½ stick melted margarine)

Preheat oven to 400° F.
Combine flour, oatmeal, baking powder, sugar, fruit, nuts.
In a separate bowl, beat egg, then stir in milk and oil.
Add liquid mixture to flour and stir until coarsely blended.
Pour into 12 muffin tins lined with paper.
Bake 15 to 20 minutes.

Carrot Muffins
1½ cups flour (whole wheat if desired)
½ cup uncooked oatmeal
½ cup brown sugar
1 tablespoon baking powder
1 cup carrots, finely shredded
¼ cup nuts (walnuts, sunflower seeds—optional)
2 eggs
¼ cup vegetable oil (or ½ stick melted margarine)
¼ cup milk

Preheat oven to 400° F.
Combine flour, oatmeal, brown sugar, and baking powder.
Add carrots and nuts.
In a separate bowl, beat eggs, then stir in oil and milk.
Add liquid mixture to flour and stir until coarsely blended.
Pour into 12 muffin tins lined with paper.
Bake 15 to 20 minutes.

Apple Muffins
2 cups flour (whole wheat if desired)
1 teaspoon cinnamon
1 tablespoon baking powder
1 egg (or 2 egg whites)
¼ cup honey (or ½ cup brown sugar)
¾ cup milk
¼ cup vegetable oil (or ½ stick melted margarine)
1 cup shredded apple

Preheat oven to 400° F.
Combine flour, cinnamon and baking powder.

In a separate bowl, beat egg, then stir in honey, milk, oil, and apples.
Add liquid mixture to flour and stir until coarsely blended.
Pour into 12 muffin tins lined with paper.
Bake 15 to 20 minutes.

Apple-Caramel Rolls

For those with more of a sweet tooth, these caramel rolls should fill the bill. However, because of the caramel frosting, they are challenging to eat while on the bike.

   ¾ cup packed brown sugar
   ½ cup + 2 tablespoons softened margarine
   36 pecan halves
   2 cups Bisquick baking mix
   ½ cup cold water
   1 cup finely chopped apple

Preheat oven to 450°F.
Place 2 teaspoons brown sugar, 2 teaspoons margarine, and 3 pecan halves in each of 12 muffin cups. Melt in oven.
Combine baking mix and water until soft dough forms, then beat vigorously for 20 strokes.
Smooth dough into a ball on floured board.
Knead 5 times.
Roll dough into a rectangle (approx. 15 x 9 inches).
Spread 2 tablespoons margarine, ¼ cup brown sugar, and apple on the rectangle of dough. Roll up tightly.
Cut into twelve 1¼-inch-wide slices.
Place slices, cut side down, in muffin cups.
Bake 10 minutes.
Invert immediately on a heatproof serving plate.

Beverage Recipes

In addition to natural fruit juices, there are many ready-made commercial drinks (Table 8.2.). Two easy-to-prepare fluid favorites are the following:

Kool-aid—Add ¼ of the amount of sugar suggested on the package instructions and up to ¼ teaspoon salt per quart.

Tea—Use any regular green or black tea or, if you prefer, a spiced or herb tea. Sweeten to taste with up to ¼ cup sugar per quart.

Shakes and Smoothies

These provide not only fluid replacement but are also high in carbohydrate Calories. As they are semiliquid, they are readily emptied from the stomach and provide a pleasant-tasting energy boost on a long ride. Two examples are:

Cathy's Banana Shake

½ cup orange juice
½ cup pineapple juice
touch of honey
2 bananas

Blend on high

Chris's Fruit Frosty

cranberry juice
orange juice
strawberries
pineapple chunks
bananas
frozen fruit bars (grape or strawberry)
ice cubes

Blend on high

Appetizer and Soup Recipes

Gazpacho
    3 large ripe tomatoes
    1 red pepper
    1 medium yellow onion
    1 large shallot
    1 large cucumber
    ¼ cup red wine vinegar
    ¼ cup olive oil
    ¾ cup canned tomato juice
    1 egg, lightly beaten
    cayenne pepper, salt, black pepper
    ¼ cup chopped fresh dill

Wash, core, and coarsely chop vegetables.
Seed cucumber.
Mix vinegar, olive oil, canned tomato juice, and egg.
Using a blender or food processor, puree vegetables.
Add vinegar mixture.
Add cayenne, black pepper, and salt to taste.
Chill.

Serves 4

Vichyssoise
    3 tablespoons unsalted butter
    4 large leeks, whites only, thinly sliced
    1 small yellow onion, thinly sliced
    4 potatoes, peeled and thinly sliced
    3 cups chicken stock
    ¾ tablespoon lemon juice
    1½ cup milk
    2 cups whipping cream
    pepper, salt

Melt butter and sauté leeks and onion.
Add potatoes, chicken stock, and lemon juice.
Boil for 1 hour. Cool.
Process in food processor or blender.
Return to pot. Add milk and one half of the cream.

Season to taste with pepper and salt.
Bring to a simmer for 1 minute.
Remove from heat, cool and then refrigerate.
Add remaining cream just prior to serving.

Serves 6

Lemon Soup

8 cups chicken broth
4 eggs
juice of 2 lemons
salt and pepper

Heat broth—simmer 20 minutes.
Beat eggs and lemon juice together until well blended.
Pour into broth slowly while stirring—do not boil.
Heat until thickened—do not boil.
Season to taste. Chill and serve.

Serves 8

Mushroom Salad with Mustard Vinaigrette

¼ cup Dijon style mustard
¼ cup wine vinegar
½ teaspoon dried oregano, crushed
¼ teaspoon salt
¼ teaspoon pepper
½ cup olive oil or salad oil
12 oz (4½ cups) fresh mushrooms, sliced
½ cup pitted olives, halved

Combine mustard, vinegar, oregano, salt, and pepper in a large bowl.
Using a whisk, blend in oil.
Stir in mushrooms and olives.
Cover and chill at least 2 hours.
May be served with tomato slices and watercress sprig.

Serves 4

Carrot-Yogurt Salad

1 lb carrots, coarsely shredded
2 medium apples, grated
1 cup yogurt
1 tablespoon honey (optional)
juice from one lemon
salt, pepper
1 tablespoon sesame seeds (optional)
¼ cup sunflower seeds, almonds, cashews (optional)
½ cup celery, finely minced (optional)
½ cup pineapple (optional)

Combine ingredients.
Chill.

Serves 4

Cole Slaw

4 cups cabbage, finely shredded
2 carrots, grated
½ cup yogurt
½ cup mayonnaise
3 tablespoons vinegar
salt, pepper
½ cup green pepper, minced (optional)
½ cup red onion, thinly sliced (optional)

Combine ingredients.
Chill several hours before serving.

Serves 6

* Fresh Fruit Salad *

1 small container yogurt or sour cream
1 apple
1 small package raisins
1 small package shredded coconut (optional)
1 banana
1 package ground nuts (optional)

Core and chop apple.
Peel and slice banana.

Mix all ingredients with sour cream or yogurt.

Serves 2

* Fresh Vegie Salad *

Fresh seasonal vegetables as available, such as:
carrots, celery, cauliflower, broccoli, radishes, tomatoes
1 small head of lettuce (optional)
1 small bottle salad dressing of your choice

Chop vegetables and lettuce.
Add dressing.

Serves 1 or more, depending on quantities used

Richard's Paté

1 large onion
1 stick celery
½ teaspoon garlic, crushed
¾ lb chicken livers
½ lb white meat of chicken
¼ cup walnuts, toasted
¼ cup raisins
2 teaspoons paté spice (see next recipe)
2 tablespoons Madeira
2 tablespoons cognac
¼ lb unsalted butter

Grate onion and celery in food processor.
Sauté onion, celery, and garlic with one third of the butter.
Return to the food processor (use steel blade).
Sauté chicken livers with one third of the butter and add to food processor.
Sauté white meat of chicken. Add to food processor.
Add walnuts, raisins, paté spice, Madeira, cognac, and remainder of butter to the food processor.
Blend until coarsely mixed, place in paté pan.
Refrigerate.
Serve with French baguettes (crusty bread) and unsalted butter.
Cornichons (small French pickles) add a nice extra touch.

Serves 8–12 as an appetizer, 4–6 as a light meal

Paté Spice (for preceding recipe)
1 teaspoon bay leaves
1½ teaspoon thyme
1½ teaspoon rosemary
1½ teaspoon basil
2½ teaspoon cinnamon
1½ teaspoon mace
¾ teaspoon ground cloves
¼ teaspoon allspice
½ teaspoon ground white pepper
1 teaspoon paprika

Mix herbs and finely crush them in a spice mortar.
Sift through fine sieve.
Add powdered spices.
Store in a tightly closed jar.

* Raw Vegetables *
Use any crisp vegetables that can be eaten uncooked, such as:
carrots
celery
broccoli
cauliflower
radishes

Wash.
Remove inedible portions.
Cut into easily manageable pieces.

* Fresh Fruit *
Use fresh seasonal fruit as available, such as:
apples
grapes
melons

Wash.
Remove rind or skins that would be difficult on the bike.
Core, if appropriate, and cut into manageable pieces.
Serve with cheese if desired.

Chilled Braised Asparagus with Vinaigrette
   1 bunch asparagus (1 pound)
   pan of ice water
   vinaigrette (see next recipe)

Bring pot of salted water to a boil.
Drop in asparagus spears.
Cook until desired tenderness—don't overcook.
When tender, transfer to ice water.
Stand until cool, drain, and pat dry.
Refrigerate for 1 day maximum.
Add vinaigrette prior to serving.

Serves 4

Vinaigrette (for preceding recipe)
   1 tablespoon Dijon style mustard
   4 tablespoons red wine vinegar
   1 teaspoon granulated sugar
   ½ teaspoon salt
   ½ teaspoon ground black pepper
   ½ cup olive oil

Whisk mustard with vinegar, sugar, salt, and pepper.
Add olive oil while continuing to whisk.
Adjust seasonings to taste.

Makes 1 cup

Eric's Soft Pretzels

This makes a good fresh bread to eat with any of the above recipes.

  1 package yeast
  1½ cups warm water
  1 teaspoon salt
  1 tablespoon sugar
  4 cups flour
  1 egg, beaten
  coarse salt

Preheat oven to 425° F.
Measure warm water into large bowl. Add yeast.
Add sugar, salt, and flour.
Mix and knead.
Form pretzels and place on a greased cookie sheet.
Brush with egg and sprinkle with coarse salt.
Bake 12 to 15 minutes.

Serves 4–6 (depending on how far you've ridden)

Main Course Recipes

Though the first two recipes in this section are salads in concept, they are really light meals in their own right.

Larry's Artichoke Pasta Salad

This is only one of many pasta salad options—vary this recipe using your imagination and the ingredients at hand.

    4 oz (about 1 cup) of medium-size pasta
    1 jar (6 oz) marinated artichoke hearts
    ¼ lb small mushrooms
    1 cup cherry tomatoes, halved
    1 cup medium-size ripe pitted olives
    ½ teaspoon dry basil leaves
    salt, pepper

Cook pasta, drain, rinse with cold water, and drain again.
Mix pasta, artichokes with their liquid, mushrooms, tomatoes, olives, and basil in a large bowl.
Toss gently.
Refrigerate for at least 4 hours.
Season with salt and pepper to taste before serving.

Serves 6

Aunt Jan's High-Fiber Rice Salad
    ⅓ cup pinenuts
    ⅓ cup almonds
    ⅓ cup hazelnuts
    ⅓ cup pumpkin seeds
    1 cup wild rice
    1 cup brown rice
    ½ cup sliced green onions
    ½ cup celery
    ½ cup currants
    ½ cup nonfat yogurt
    wine vinegar
    olive oil
    cayenne pepper (very important) and salt

Toast and then coarsely chop pinenuts, almonds, hazelnuts, and pumpkin seeds.
Cook rice. Drain.
Mix nuts, rice, onions, celery, and currants.
Add wine vinegar, olive oil, cayenne pepper, and salt to the yogurt. Vary to your taste.
Add yogurt dressing to rice mixture.
Serve with pita bread.

Serves 2–4

Split Pea–Parmesan Spread

    1 cup cooked green split peas
    2 tablespoons mayonnaise
    2 tablespoons Parmesan cheese
    2 tablespoons lowfat cottage cheese
    ½ teaspoon salt
    1 teaspoon dry onion flakes

Mash split peas.
Mix with other ingredients.
Serve with pita bread.

Serves 2

Grilled Lemon Chicken

    1 chicken, quartered or cut up
    1 lemon, sliced
    3 cloves garlic, crushed
    ½ cup oil, preferably olive oil
    salt and pepper

The day before serving, marinate chicken in a shallow pan with lemon, oil, salt, and pepper.
Grill over charcoal.
May be served chilled or warm. Travels well.

Serves 4

Chicken, Cheese, and Chile Rolls à la Bruce

    2 whole chicken breasts, halved
    ½ cup dry sherry
    2½ cups chicken broth
    4 tablespoons prepared mustard
    ½ teaspoon garlic salt
    pinch of dried sage, basil, and thyme
    4 large slices jack cheese
    4 strips canned peeled green chiles
    4 frozen puff pastry shells
    1 egg white, beaten
    sesame seeds

Poach chicken breasts about 20 minutes in sherry and broth.
Cool in poaching liquid for 30 minutes.
Remove skin and bones, then refrigerate.
Mix mustard and dry seasonings.
Spread 1 tablespoon of mixture over each piece of chicken.
Wrap a slice of cheese and chile around each piece.
Let puff pastry stand at room temperature for 30 minutes.
Roll each shell into an 8-inch circle (on lightly floured board).
Place piece of wrapped chicken on shell, seam side down; bring
up sides of pastry, overlap, moisten, and pinch.
Place bundles, seam down, on ungreased cookie sheet.
Brush with egg whites and sprinkle with seeds.
Chill 30 minutes.
Bake at 425° F for 30 minutes or until brown and crisp.
Cool on rack.
Chill and serve.

Makes 4

Sandwich and Quick Meal Recipes

* Sandwiches *

Here are a few examples of suitable sandwiches for eating on the bike or at the picnic site. Be guided by your own imagination and the contents of your bread bin and refrigerator (or what's available along the way).

cream cheese on brown bread
cream cheese and cucumbers on crustless white bread
Swiss or Dutch cheese on French bread or brown bread
pastrami and Swiss on rye
roast beef on white bread

* Cracker Sandwiches *

Crackers or similar crisp breads can be used instead of bread for a large variety of crunchy sandwiches. Again, here are just a few examples, to get you started. Butter or margarine may be helpful in bonding the various ingredients together if they are hard cheeses, such as Swiss, Dutch or American non-processed cheese. Use the bread of your choice with any of the following:

soft or hard cheese
cream cheese and jelly
processed cheese and jelly
salami and cheese

Cold Baked Potatoes

Baked potatoes may be the ultimate high-carbohydrate snack or main meal course. They are easy to make, particularly if you have a microwave, and are easy to carry. If you intend to eat on the bike, you may want to remove the peel beforehand.

Make with any one of various toppings, limited only by your imagination. Unless eaten on the bike, the topping is best kept separate until it's time to eat.

Dessert Recipes

Arlene's Creamy Rice Pudding
   1 cup rice
   6 cups hot milk
   1 teaspoon salt
   2 tablespoons butter
   2 teaspoons vanilla
   2 teaspoons sugar

Place all ingredients in a pot that holds at least 8 cups.
Cook over low heat (do not boil) for 1 hour.
Remove and cool, then refrigerate.
Excellent by itself or served with seasonal fruits.

Serves 6

French Apple and Bread Pudding
   ¼ cup raisins or currants
   1 large tart cooking apple
   ¼ cup melted butter
   4 beaten eggs
   1¾ cups milk
   ½ cup heavy cream
   ½ cup sugar
   ½ teaspoon vanilla
   2 cups unseasoned croutons or stale, dried bread
   ⅓ cup slivered almonds
   ⅛ cup brown sugar

Soak raisins or currants in small amount of water.
Peel, core, and thinly slice apple.
Cook apple slices in butter until translucent, then spoon into 1½-quart casserole.
In a separate bowl, beat eggs and then add milk, cream, sugar, and vanilla.
Add croutons (cubed dried bread), currants, and remaining butter to casserole.
Stir to mix with apples.
Pour egg mixture into casserole and let stand 20 minutes.
Sprinkle with nuts and brown sugar.

Place casserole in large pan of water in oven.
Bake at 350° F for 40 minutes (or until knife comes out clean).

Serves 6

Apricot Cobbler
    1½ cups all purpose flour
    ¼ teaspoon salt
    9 tablespoons unsalted butter
    ¼ cup shortening
    2½ cups fresh ripe apricots
    1 large tart apple—peeled, cored, and sliced
    1 cup sugar

Preheat oven to 450° F.
In a food processor, process flour, salt, and 5 tablespoons of butter that has been frozen previously in small pieces.
Add ¼ cup ice water and process until dough begins to cling together—about 10 seconds.
Drop apricots in boiling water for 10 seconds, then peel, pit, and cut into ½-inch-thick slices.
Roll dough into a large circle and fit into a 1½- to 2-quart baking dish.
Place apricots into dough.
Cover with sugar and dot with 4 tablespoons butter.
Place in oven and reduce to 425 °F.
Bake for 45 minutes.

Serves 6 hungry bikers

* Fresh Fruit and Cheese *
    Use any seasonal fruits such as:
    grapes, apples, pears, plums, figs, berries, melons
    any kind of non-processed cheese

Wash fruit.
Peel and core as appropriate.
Combine fruit with cheese.
May be prepared either at home or on site.

* Yogurt with Toppings*

1 container of yogurt—plain or flavor of choice
fresh seasonal fruits as available—berries are great
granola—packaged granola cereals work well here
chopped nuts
toasted coconut

Mix yogurt with toppings of your choice.

* Berries on Shortcake *

1 package shortcakes (known as shortbread in Britain)
fresh berries as available (e.g., strawberries, raspberries, or black-
berries)
1 can whipped cream
Shortcakes are particularly durable, and the berries can be
added at the picnic site. The whipped cream really hits the spot
after you've ridden a few hours.

Appendix A. Energy Requirements of Cycling

Expressed in terms of the number of Calories ingested

1. Level Surface (E_h = Energy required–horizontal)

$$P_w = v \times [3.509 + 0.2581 \times (v)^2]$$
$$P_c = P_w / 4186.8$$
$$C_e = P_c \times T$$
$$C_i = C_e \div e = E_h$$

where:

P_w	=	power (watts)
v	=	velocity, or speed (m/sec)
P_c	=	power (Cal/sec)
T	=	time (sec)
C_e	=	Calories expended at the pedals
C_i	=	Calories ingested = E_h
e	=	efficiency of the human machine (approx. 25%)
E_h	=	energy required–horizontal

Assumptions:

75 kg rider
10 kg bike
level surface
no head wind

Definitions and conversion factors:

1 watt	=	1 joule/second
1 Cal	=	1,000 cal = 4,186.8 joules = 4,186.8 watts

2. Climbing Vertical Distance (E_v = Energy required–vertical)

$$W = F \times D$$
$$C_e = W/CF$$
$$C_i = C_e/e = E_v$$

where:

W	=	work (ft-lbs or kgm)
F	=	Force from gravity (lbs or kg)
D	=	distance vertically (ft or m)
C_e	=	Calories expended at the pedals
CF	=	conversion factor of 3,097 or 418 (for American and International units, respectively)
C_i	=	Calories ingested = E_v
e	=	efficiency of the human machine (approx. 25%)
E_v	=	energy required–vertical

Definitions and conversion factors:

1 Cal	=	1,000 cal	=	4,184.8 joules
1 joule	=	74 ft-lb	=	0.10 kgm
1 Cal	=	3,097 ft-lb	=	418 kgm

3. Total Energy Requirements in Hilly Terrain

$E_t \;=\; E_h + E_v$

where:

E_t = Total energy requirements of cycling up a hill (in Calories ingested)

E_h = Energy requirements for horizontal distance covered (in Calories ingested)

E_v = Energy requirements for vertical distance climbed (in Calories ingested)

Example:

A 165-lb cyclist (75 kg) rides a 10-mile hilly route at an average speed of 15 miles/hour (6.7 meters/sec). During the ride, he climbs 1,500 feet (457 meters). His bicycle weighs 22 lbs (10 kg). How many Calories will he need to eat to replace the energy expended?

P_w = $6.7\,[3.509 + 0.2581\,(6.7)^2]$
    = $6.7\,[3.509 + 11.586]$
    = 101 watts

P_c = $101/4{,}186.8 = 0.024$ Cal/sec

T = $10/15 = 0.66$ hour
  = $0.66 \times 3{,}600$
  = 2,376 sec

C_e = $0.024\ 2{,}376 = 57$ Cal

C_i = 57 Cal $/0.25 = 228$ Cal $= E_h$

W = 85 kg $\times 457$ meters
  = 38,845 kgm

C_e = $38{,}845/418 = 92$ Cal

C_i = $92/0.25 = 371$ Calories $= E_v$

E_t = $E_h + E_v$
    = 228 Cal $+ 371$ Cal
    = 599 Cal needed to replace those expended.

If one is a purist, 50 Cal/hour need to be added for basal metabolism.

Since this ride took ⅔ of an hour, the correct approximation is $599 + (⅔ \times 50) = 632$ Calories.

Appendix B. International Units

Scientific measurements can be expressed in several ways. English units (pound, inch) are still in common use in the United States. The rest of the world, including Britain, uses the International System of Units (SI units). The latter is based on the metric system (kilogram, centimeter) and is used in most scientific texts.

Conversion Table

1 inch	=	2.54 centimeters
1 foot	=	0.305 meters
	=	30.5 cm
1 mile	=	1.609 m
	=	1.609 km
1 mph	=	1.609 km/hr
	=	0.445 m/sec
1 ounce	=	28.35 grams
1 pound	=	454 grams (mass)
	=	4.5 N (Newton) (force)
1 quart	=	947 cubic centimeters
	=	0.947 liter
1 watt	=	1 joule/second
	=	0.014 Kilocalories/min
	=	0.014 Cal/min
1 joule	=	0.74 ft-lb
	=	1 Nm (corresponding to approximately 0.1 kgm under normal sea-level gravitational effects)
1 Calorie	=	3097 ft-lb
	=	1 kcal
	=	1,000 cal
	=	418 kgm
	=	4,184.6 joules (J)
	=	4.18 kilojoules (kJ)

absolute work:
The actual number of Calories expended to accomplish a task. It is the same for all individuals and is not affected by the level of conditioning.

adenosine diphosphate (ADP):
A coenzyme that acts as an intermediate carrier in cellular metabolism. It is transformed into ATP (see below) by the addition of a phosphate group.

adenosine triphosphate (ATP):
An organic compound acting as a carrier for intermediary energy storage during cellular metabolism. It is the last chemical compound formed in the transfer of food energy into mechanical work.

aerobic metabolism:
Cellular energy release carried out in the presence of oxygen.

anaerobic metabolism:
Cellular energy release carried out without oxygen.

basal metabolic rate (BMR):
The heat production (energy consumption) of an individual at the lowest level of cellular activity (metabolism) in the waking state.

bonk:
A descriptive term identifying that point at which liver glycogen is depleted and maximum energy output cannot be maintained. It can be delayed or reversed by eating carbohydrates.

caloric replacement:
The number of Calories that must be eaten to replace those required to carry out a certain amount of work.

calorie:
The old scientific unit of energy (superseded by the joule; see below). It is the energy required to raise the temperature of 1 gram of water 1 degree Centigrade.

Calorie:
A unit of energy equal to 1,000 calories. This is the unit used when referring to the energy content of foods as well as to the production and utilization of energy in man.

carbohydrate:
An organic compound containing carbon, hydrogen, and oxygen. It is a basic source of energy for the cell and yields 4.1 Calories per gram.

cardiac output:
The rate at which blood is pumped by the heart, usually expressed in liters/minute.

century ride:
A bicycle ride of 100 miles. There can also be a "metric" century of 100 kilometers.

chyme:
The semifluid mass of partly digested food passed from the stomach into the duodenum.

complex carbohydrate:
An organic molecule composed of at least two simple (single) carbohydrate molecules.

concentration:
The quantity of any substance in a defined volume of a solution or mixture.

disaccharide:
A carbohydrate consisting of two molecules.

diuretic:
A compound which promotes water excretion by the kidneys.

efficiency:
The ratio of work output to energy input.

energy:
The capacity for doing work.

essential:
Necessary. In the context of nutrition, this refers to basic food elements (fats and amino acids) that cannot be synthesized by the body. These substances are each necessary for cellular metabolism and existence, making them also essential components of the diet.

exhaustion:
The point at which the athlete cannot maintain an initial level of activity, even with an adequate blood glucose supply. Related to a change in the muscle itself—not the source of energy.

fatigue:
The point at which the body's glucose stores are depleted and all energy is derived from fat metabolism. It can be reversed with oral glucose supplements.

fatty acid (FA):
One of the molecules making up a triglyceride, the basic component of fatty tissue, and an essential intermediary in fat metabolism.

fluid deficit:
The difference between the body's ideal water content and it's actual water content (usually after exercise).

fructose:
Fruit sugar. Important, as it can be metabolized to glycogen without insulin.

gluconeogenesis:
The production of glucose, a carbohydrate, from either fat or protein. It is often an intermediate step in energy production from these materials.

glucose:
The monosaccharide that is the most important carbohydrate in cellular metabolism.

glycogen:
The form in which carbohydrate is stored in the body. When needed, it is converted in the tissues into glucose.

hitting the wall:
A descriptive term identifying that point at which both liver and muscle glycogen have been depleted and maximum energy output cannot be maintained. It can be delayed by eating carbohydrates while exercising,

but cannot be reversed once it occurs.

international units:
See SI units.

joule:
The scientific unit of energy—see the conversion table in Appendix B for the equivalent in calories and Calories.

lactic acid:
One of the by-products of anaerobic metabolism. It has a negative effect on muscle functioning and, in this way, limits athletic performance.

maximal oxygen consumption (V_{O2max}):
The maximum amount (volume) of oxygen that an individual can consume in a set period of time (l/min). It can also be expressed per kilogram of body weight (ml/kg/min). It is a reflection of the upper limit of aerobic metabolism and is a product of the maximal cardiac output and maximal arterial-venous oxygen difference.

maximum heart rate (MHR):
The maximum attainable heart rate for an individual. It decreases with age and can be estimated using the formula: MHR = 220 − (age in years).

metabolism:
The biochemical cellular functions involved in energy production.

minerals:
Inorganic elements or compounds that are essential constituents of all cells.

mitochrondria:
The component of the cell where glucose, fat, or protein are oxidized to release energy for cell activities.

monosaccharide:
A carbohydrate consisting of a single molecule.

osmotic activity:
Relating to the concentration (number of molecules in a given volume) of a solution.

oxidation:
Literally, the chemical combination with oxygen, releasing energy in the process.

oxygen consumption (V_{O2}):
The total volume of oxygen consumed by the cells of the body over a given period of time in carrying out the basic metabolic functions.

oxygen debt:
The amount of oxygen required for the removal of the lactic acid and other metabolic products that accumulate during anaerobic metabolism.

paceline:
Several cyclists drafting (following closely) one another in a line to minimize energy needs and improve the performance of the group.

placebo:
An inactive compound given for suggestive effect.

polymer:
A substance made up of a chain of similar units. In the context of this text, it refers to a chain of simple glucose molecules.

power:
The rate at which work is done. For example, if an 80-kg bicycle and rider are raised 3 meters in 1 minute, power is expressed as 240 kg-meters per minute (kgm/h).

relative work rate:
The percentage of a person's V_{O2max} required to accomplish a task. Even though the absolute work is the same for all riders, the relative work rate can vary from individual to individual, depending on the level of conditioning.

second wind:
The phenomenon of easing of effort for any given level of exercise which occurs after warming up. It is thought to relate, in some degree, to a shift from carbohydrate toward fat metabolism in the cell.

SI units (international units):
The international system of units (as opposed to the English system) based on the metric system. In nutritional literature, the English system remains widely accepted in the United States.

trace element:
Any mineral supplied by the food that is only present in the body in a minute concentration.

triglyceride:
The basic molecule of fat (adipose) tissue. Triglycerides contain 9.3 Calories per gram.

urea:
The end product of protein metabolism in man, which is excreted.

V_{O2max}:
See maximal oxygen consumption.

work:
The application of a force over a (vertical) distance. For example, moving 80 kg up over a distance of 2 meters equals 160 kg-meters (kgm) of work.

Bibliography

1. Anderson, J. and B.L. Becker. "Carbohydrate Power." *Rx Being Well* (Sept./Oct. 1987): 41–45.

2. Askew, E.W. "Role of Fat Metabolism in Exercise." *Clinics in Sports Medicine* 3 (July 1984): 605–621.

3. Burke, E., H.R. Perez, and P. Hodges. *Inside the Cyclist.* Battleboro: Velo News, 1986.

4. Casal, D.C., and A.S. Leon. "Metabolic Effects of Caffeine on Submaximal Exercise Performance in Marathoners." *Med. Sci. Sports Exer.* 14 (1982): 176

5. Coggan, A.R. and E.F. Coyle. "Reversal of Fatigue During Prolonged Exercise by Carbohydrate Infusion or Ingestion." *J. Appl. Physiol.* 63 (1987): 2388–2395.

6. Costill, D.L. "Carbohydrates for Exercise: Dietary Demands for Optimal Performance." *Int. J. Sports Med.* 9 (1988): 1–18.

7. Costill, D.L. "Water and Electrolyte Requirements During Exercise." *Clinics in Sports Medicine* 3 (July 1984): 639–648.

8. Costill, D.L., W. M. Sherman, W.J. Fink et al. "The Role of Dietary Carbohydrates in Muscle Glycogen Resynthesis after Strenuous Running." *Amer. J. Clin. Nutr.* 34 (1981): 1831–1836.

9. Coyle, E.F. "Ergogenic Aids." *Clinics in Sports Medicine* 3 (July 1984): 731–742.

10. Coyle, E.F. personal communication.

11. Coyle, E.F., A.R. Coggan, M.K. Hemmert et al. "Muscle Glycogen Utilization During Prolonged Strenuous Exercise When Fed Carbohydrate." *J. Appl. Physiol.* 61 (1986): 165–172.

12. Coyle, E.F., A.R. Coggan, M.K. Hemmert, R.C. Lowe, and T.J. Walters. "Substrate Usage During Prolonged Exercise Following a Pre-exercise Meal." *J. Appl. Physiol.* 59 (1985): 429–433.

13. Dohm, G.L. "Protein Nutrition for the Athlete." Clinics in Sports Medicine 3 (July 1984): 595–604.

14. Dohm, G.L., R.T. Beeker, R.G. Israel, and E.B. Tapscott. "Metabolic Responses to Exercise after Fasting." *J. Appl. Physiol.* 61 (1986): 1363–1368.

15. Elliot, D.L., and L. Goldberg. "Nutrition and Exercise." *Med. Clin. N. Amer.* 69 (1985): 71–82.

16. "Exercise Slows GI Transit." *Gastroenterology Observer* 6 (1987): 7.

17. Faria, I.E. "Applied Physiology of Cycling." *Sports Medicine* 1 (1984): 187–204.

18. Gollnick, P.D., and H. Matoba. "Role of Carbohydrate in Exercise." *Clinics in Sports Medicine* 3 (July 1984): 583–593.

19. Dr. Gwinup, Divn. of Endocrinology and Metabolism, UC Irvine Med. Ctr., as presented

at 37th. Annual Obesity and Assoc. Cond. Symposium.

20. Hargreaves, M., D.L. Costill, A. Coggan, I. Nishibata, and W.J. Fink. "Carbohydrate Feedings and Exercise Performance." *Med. Sci. Sports Exer.* 15 (1983): 129.

21. Hecker, A.L. "Nutritional Conditioning." *Clinics in Sports Medicine* 3 (July 1984): 567–582.

22. Higdon, H. "Breakfast (Lunch and Dinner) of Champions." *Hippocrates* 2 (1988): 44–58.

23. Holloszy, J.O., M.J. Rennie, R.C. Hickson et al. "Physiologic Consequences of the Biochemical Adaptations to Endurance Exercise." *Ann. NY Acad. Sci.* 301 (1977): 440–450.

24. Ivy, J.L., D.L. Costill, J.W. Fink, and R.W. Lower. "Influence of Caffeine and Carbohydrate Feedings on Endurance Performance." *Med. and Science in Sports* 11 (1979): 6–11.

25. Ivy, J.L., A.L. Katz, C.L. Cutler et al. "Muscle Glycogen Synthesis After Exercise: Effect of Time of Carbohydrate Ingestion." *J. Appl. Physiol.* 64 (1988): 1480–1485.

26. Karlsson, J., and B. Saltin. "Diet, Muscle Glycogen, and Endurance Performance." *J. App. Phys.* 31 (1971): 203–206.

27. Larson, E.B., and R.A. Bruce. "Editorial: Exercise and Aging." *Ann. of Int. Med.* 105 (November 1986): 783–785.

28. Locksley, R. "Fuel Utilization in Marathons: Implications for Performance." *West. J. Med.* 133 (1980): 493–502.

29. Loy, S.F., R.K. Conlee, W.W. Winder, A.G. Nelson, D.A. Arnall, and A.G. Fisher. "Effects of 24 Hour Fast on Cycling Endurance Time at Two Different Intensities." *J. Appl. Physiol.* 61 (1986): 654–659.

30. Merkin, G. "Eating for Competition." *Seminars in Adolescent Medicine* 3 (1987): 177–183.

31. Meyers, F., and R.S. Fischer. "A Rational Approach to Gastric Emptying Disorders." *International Medicine* 9 (1988): 112–122.

32. Morella, J.J., and R.J. Turchetti. *Nutrition and the Athlete.* Van Nostrand Reinhold Company, 1982.

33. Neufer, P.D., D.L. Costill, M.G. Flynn, J.P. Kirwan, J.B. Mitchell, and J. Houmard. "Improvements in Exercise Performance: Effects of Carbohydrate Feedings and Diet." *J. Appl. Physiol.* 62 (1987): 983–988.

34. Pena, N. "Legal Performance Enhancers." *Bicycling* 28 (July 1987): 30–34.

35. Pena, N. "What Does this Man Know that You Don't? " *Bicycling* 19 (1988): 73–77.

36. "Position of the American Dietetic Association: Nutrition for Physical Fitness and Athletic Performance for Adults." *J. Am. Dietetic Assoc.* 87 (1987): 933–939.

37. Powers, S.K., R.J. Byrd, R. Tulley, and T. Calender. "Effects of Caffeine Ingestion on Metabolism and Performance During Graded Exercise." *Med. Sci. Sports Exer.* 14 (1982): 176.

38. Pritikin, N. *Diet for Runners.* New York: Simon and Schuster, 1982.

39. *Recommended Dietary Allowances.* National Academy of Sciences, 1980.

40. Roedde, S., J.D. MacDougall, J.R. Sutton, and H.J. Green. "Supercompensation of Muscle Glycogen in Trained and Untrained Subjects." *Canad. J. Appl. Sports Sciences* 11 (1986): 42–46.

41. Schoene, R.B. "Nutrition for Ultra-endurance: Several Hours to Several Months." *Clinics in Sports Medicine* 3 (July 1984): 679–692.

42. Simons-Morton, B.G., R.R. Pate, and D.G. Simons-Morton. "Prescribing Physical Activity to Prevent Disease." *Postgraduate Medicine* 83 (1988): 165–176.

43. Smith, N.J. "Weight Control in the Athlete." *Clinics in Sports Medicine* 3 (July 1984): 693–704.

44. White, J., and M.A. Ford. "The Hydration and Electrolyte Maintenance Properties of an Experimental Sports Drink." *Brit. J. Sports Medicine* 17 (1983): 51–58.

45. White, J.A., C. Ward, and H. Nelson. "Ergogenic Demands of a 24-Hour Cycling Event." *Brit. J. Sports Medicine* 18 (1984): 165–171.

46. Whitney, E.N. *Nutrition—Concepts and Controversies.* West Publishing Company, 1982.

47. Whitt, F.R., and D.G. Wilson. *Bicycling Science.* Cambridge: MIT Press, 1982.

48. Williams, M.H. "Vitamin and Mineral Supplements to Athletes: Do They Help?" *Clinics in Sports Medicine* 3 (July 1984): 623–637.

49. Wilmore, J.H., and B.J. Freund. "Nutritional Enhancement of Athletic Performance." *Current Concepts in Nutrition* 15 (1986): 67–97.

50. Young, V.R. "Protein and Amino Acid Metabolism in Relation to Physical Exercise." *Current Concepts in Nutrition* 15 (1986): 9–32.

51. Zahradnik, F. "Sports Drinks." *Bicycling* 28 (September 1987): 46–50.

52. Zanecosky, A. "Nutrition for Athletes." *Clinics in Podiatric Medicine and Surgery* 3 (1986): 623–630.

200. McCole, S.D., K. Claney, J. Conte et al. "Energy Expenditure During Bicycling." *J. Appl. Physiol.* 68 (1990): 748–753.

201. Coyle, E.F., A.R. Coggan, M.K. Hopper, and T.J. Walters. "Determinants of Endurance in Well Trained Cyclists." *J. Appl. Physiol.* 64 (1988): 2622–2630.

203. O'Toole, M.L., P.S. Douglas, W.D.B. Hiller. "Applied

Physiology of a Triathlon." *Sports Medicine* 8 (1989): 201–225.

204. Pierce, E.F., A. Weltman, R.L. Seip, and D. Snead. "Effects of Training Specificity on the Lactate Threshold and V$_{O2}$ Peak." *Int. J. Sports Med.* 11 (1990): 267–272.

205. Schneider, D.A., K.A. LaCroix, G.R. Atkinson, P.J. Troped, and J. Pollack. "Ventilatory Threshold and Maximal Oxygen Uptake During Cycling and Running in Triathletes." *Med. Sci. Sports Exer.* 22 (1990): 257–264.

206. King. A.C., B. Frey-Hewitt, D.M. Dreon, and P.D. Wood. "Diet vs Exercise in Weight Maintenance." *Arch. Int. Med.* 142 (1989): 2741–2746.

207. Sherman, W.M., G. Brodowicz, D.A. Wright, W.K. Allen, J. Simonsen, and A. Dernbach. "Effects of 4 Hour Pre-exercise Carbohydrate Feedings on Cycling Performance." *Med Sci. Sports Exer.* 21 (1989): 598–604.

208. Ivy, J.L. "Effect of Amount of a Carbohydrate Supplement on a Rapid Glycogen Resynthesis Post Exercise." *J. Appl. Physiol.* 1988: In Press.

209. Coyle, E.F., J.M. Hagberg, B.F. Hurley, W.H. Martin, A.A. Ehsani, and J.O. Holloszy. "Carbohydrate Feeding During Prolonged Strenuous Exercise Can Delay Fatigue." *J. Appl. Physiol.* 55 (1983): 230–235

210. Stewart, I., L. McNaughton, P. Davies, and S. Tristan. "Phosphate Loading and the Effects on V$_{O2max}$ in Trained Cyclists." *Research Quarterly for Exercise and Sport* 61 (1990): 80–84.

211. Saris, W.H.M., M.A. van Erp-Baart, F. Brouns, K.R. Westerterp, and F. ten Hoor. "Study on Food Intake and Energy Expenditure During Extreme Sustained Exercise: The Tour de France." *Int J. Sports Med.* 10 (1989): S26–S31.

212. Brouns, F., W.H.M. Saris, J. Stroecken, E. Beckers, R. Thijssen, N.J. Reher, and F. ten Hoor. "A Controlled Tour de France Simulation Study: Part 1 and Part 2." *Int. J. Sports Med.* 10 (1989): S32–S48.

213. Brouns, F., W.H.M. Saris, E. Beckers, H. Adlercreutz, G.J. van der Vusse, H.A. Kreizer, H. Kuipers, P. Menheere, A.J.M. Wagenmakers, and F. ten Hoor. "Metabolic Changes Induced by Sustained Exhaustive Cycling and Diet Manipulation." *Int. J. Sports Med.* 10 (1989): 49–S62.

Other Books Published by Bicycle Books

Bicycle Books has published numerous books about the bicycle and cycling.

Our books are available in many bike shops and book shops.
Book shops can obtain our titles for you from our book trade
distributor (National Book Network for the USA) or from some
of the major wholesalers, bike shops directly from us.

If you have difficulty obtaining our books elsewhere, we will
be pleased to supply them by mail.

To receive our free catalog and price list, call or write:

Bicycle Books, Inc.   In Britain: Bicycle Books
PO Box 2038   463 Ashley Road
Mill Valley CA 94941 (USA)   Poole, Dorset BH14 0AX
Tel. (415) 381-0172   Tel. (0202) 71 53 49